5-Star Re

years. Technology and globalization have had a significant impact on many aspects of our lives, including the way we work. If you have not been able to keep up with the new trends but want to run a successful business, I recommend that you read Vibrant Publishers' Organizational Behavior Essentials You Always Wanted to Know. In this volume (an incredible mine of information), you will have at your disposal valuable material on development theories, how to manage diversity and inclusion, how to motivate your team, and much, much more. Additionally, Organizational Behavior Essentials You Always Wanted to Know includes a very useful glossary, quizzes, and summaries for each chapter.

It is rare to find a book that helps its readers in a significant way, but Organizational Behavior Essentials You Always Wanted to Know does this and more. Vibrant Publishers has done an excellent job of researching and analyzing the issues that interest everyone who wants to run a successful organization. I particularly like that Vibrant Publishers stresses the importance of creating the best possible atmosphere in the workplace. Moreover, I appreciate how they emphasize the positive impact that diversity brings to every company. Overall, Organizational Behavior Essentials You Always Wanted to Know is very well-balanced and clear, and the chapter summaries and quizzes are helpful. After reading this book, readers will not doubt what is worth doing for the success of their organization. I recommend it to anyone who wants to remain competitive in the market.

This review is for an earlier edition.

This page is intentionally left blank

SELF-LEARNING MANAGEMENT SERIES

ORGANIZATIONAL BEHAVIOR ESSENTIALS

YOU ALWAYS WANTED TO KNOW

SECOND EDITION

A practical guide for mastering the three levels of organizational behavior.

VIC CLESCERI

Organizational Behavior Essentials You Always Wanted To Know

Second Edition

Paperback ISBN 10: 1-63651-230-5
Paperback ISBN 13: 978-1-63651-230-3

Ebook ISBN 10: 1-63651-231-3
Ebook ISBN 13: 978-1-63651-231-0

Hardback ISBN 10: 1-63651-232-1
Hardback ISBN 13: 978-1-63651-232-7

Library of Congress Control Number: 2021936892

This publication is designed to provide accurate and authoritative information in regard to the subject matter covered. The Author has made every effort in the preparation of this book to ensure the accuracy of the information. However, information in this book is sold without warranty either expressed or implied. The Author or the Publisher will not be liable for any damages caused or alleged to be caused either directly or indirectly by this book.

Vibrant Publishers books are available at special quantity discount for sales promotions, or for use in corporate training programs. For more information please write to bulkorders@vibrantpublishers.com

Please email feedback / corrections (technical, grammatical or spelling) to spellerrors@vibrantpublishers.com

To access the complete catalogue of Vibrant Publishers, visit www.vibrantpublishers.com

SELF-LEARNING MANAGEMENT SERIES

TITLE	PAPERBACK* ISBN
ACCOUNTING, FINANCE & ECONOMICS	
COST ACCOUNTING AND MANAGEMENT ESSENTIALS	9781636511030
FINANCIAL ACCOUNTING ESSENTIALS	9781636510972
FINANCIAL MANAGEMENT ESSENTIALS	9781636511009
MACROECONOMICS ESSENTIALS	9781636511818
MICROECONOMICS ESSENTIALS	9781636511153
PERSONAL FINANCE ESSENTIALS	9781636511849

ENTREPRENEURSHIP & STRATEGY	
BUSINESS COMMUNICATION ESSENTIALS	9781636511634
BUSINESS PLAN ESSENTIALS	9781636511214
BUSINESS STRATEGY ESSENTIALS	9781949395778
ENTREPRENEURSHIP ESSENTIALS	9781636511603

GENERAL MANAGEMENT	
BUSINESS LAW ESSENTIALS	9781636511702
DATA ANALYTICS ESSENTIALS	9781636511184
DECISION MAKING ESSENTIALS	9781636510026
LEADERSHIP ESSENTIALS	9781636510316
PRINCIPLES OF MANAGEMENT ESSENTIALS	9781636511542
TIME MANAGEMENT ESSENTIALS	9781636511665

*Also available in Hardback & Ebook formats

SELF-LEARNING MANAGEMENT SERIES

TITLE	PAPERBACK* ISBN

HUMAN RESOURCE MANAGEMENT

Title	ISBN
DIVERSITY IN THE WORKPLACE ESSENTIALS	9781636511122
HR ANALYTICS ESSENTIALS	9781636510347
HUMAN RESOURCE MANAGEMENT ESSENTIALS	9781949395839
ORGANIZATIONAL BEHAVIOR ESSENTIALS	9781636512303
ORGANIZATIONAL DEVELOPMENT ESSENTIALS	9781636511481

MARKETING & SALES MANAGEMENT

Title	ISBN
DIGITAL MARKETING ESSENTIALS	9781949395747
MARKETING MANAGEMENT ESSENTIALS	9781636511788
SALES MANAGEMENT ESSENTIALS	9781636510743
SERVICES MARKETING ESSENTIALS	9781636511733
SOCIAL MEDIA MARKETING ESSENTIALS	9781636512181

OPERATIONS & PROJECT MANAGEMENT

Title	ISBN
AGILE ESSENTIALS	9781636510057
OPERATIONS & SUPPLY CHAIN MANAGEMENT ESSENTIALS	9781949395242
PROJECT MANAGEMENT ESSENTIALS	9781636510712
STAKEHOLDER ENGAGEMENT ESSENTIALS	9781636511511

*Also available in Hardback & Ebook formats

About the Author

For more than thirty years, **Vic Clesceri** has dedicated his career to developing and leading people. He has done this within boardrooms, conference rooms, and classrooms, as a management executive, professor, consultant, and certified coach. Vic is passionate about serving people by helping them develop to their fullest potential, both personally and professionally.

Vic brings a diverse background and experience in talent management and organizational development, having led people and teams across many industries, including food and beverage, dairy, pharmaceuticals, nonprofits, education, and professional services. He has led talent management and organizational development initiatives across many disparate business functions, including sales, strategy, analytics, customer development, and business planning. Vic's experience in this space has also served organizations from $5 million to $15 billion.

Vic is the Founder and Leader Sherpa of The Management Sherpa, a boutique talent management and organizational development consultancy. He works as both an executive coach and business advisor within these spaces. In addition to this professional work, Vic is a Visiting Assistant Professor with Miami University's Farmer School of Business and an adjunct faculty member for Mount St. Joseph University's Master of Science in Organizational Leadership program, where he teaches courses in Talent Management & Development, Organizational Behavior, and Change Management. Vic holds an MBA from Webster University and an MAEd from Central Michigan University.

What experts say about this book!

This book provides an exploration of how managers and employees work in groups for the completion of organizational objectives. Emphasis is placed on the growing dependency on understanding the behavior and personality of communities of practice (teams) in the workplace. The textbook equips students with insights regarding the ability to manage work teams, operate and navigate teams successfully, and obtain successful results via team dynamics. Researchers tell us that opportunities to succeed need to be more abundant in today's workplaces; the author of this book is the proverbial knock and invitation for students to open that door.

– Fernán R. Cepero
Organizational & Global Leader

(1) The study of *Organizational Behavior* is complex. Yet, this well-written textbook titled *"Organizational Behavior Essentials"* makes it easy for a student to master the subject matter in a textbook using the self-study method; (2) Students take a quiz at the end of each chapter. This ensures students' success in mastering organizational behavior; (3) Answers are provided for each quiz making it easy for a student to self-evaluate after its completion; (4) the textbook is in a focused style and written examples are provided for each concept for the student. As the textbook is illustrated with examples, a student is expected to learn the concepts easily. Overall, excellent writing and format of the textbook, and the price is right.

– Dr. Benito Garza
South Texas College

What experts say about this book!

This book will be an industry standard on how you provide a blueprint for creating a more sustainable and equitable work environment. The four major areas that are important for readers to understand are: A) Culture and Communication; B) Diversity and Inclusion; C) High Performance Work Teams, and D) Talent Development. Organizational Behavior Essential Matters! It will provide a strategic developmental framework for re-invigorating your employees to high-level success.

– Denean Robinson
Instructor of Workforce Continuing Education

Organizational Behavior Essentials provides a concise guide in helping the reader understand the components of organizations as well as identify what makes a successful organization. This includes leadership character, the importance of high-performance teams, the need for talent development and training, successfully communicating the need for change, and employee relations. All subjects address the increasing globalization of the workplace and the need for a diverse and multicultural approach to be successful. This book is well-written, very clear, and very helpful for someone who wants an overview of what is meant by organizational behavior. I liked the importance it placed on leadership character, training, and development. A minor plus for me was the acknowledgment that high-performance teams also need a sense of empathy and inclusiveness or else they would create a very negative workplace atmosphere.

– Jeff Conner
Library Director, Command Fleet Activities Yokosuka (CFAY), Japan

What experts say about this book!

Organizational Behavior is a vast subject of study and it requires a comprehensive and holistic approach to understand it. This book has nicely presented the essential concepts of Organizational Behavior in easy language for the students of management programs. The quizzes at the end of the chapters are helpful in self-assessments. All essential and relevant aspects related to Organizational Behavior are considered in this book and it is useful for practitioners too.

– Anant Kumar Srivastava
Professor- Information Systems and Analytics,Asia-Pacific Institute of Management, New Delhi

It is important to have reliable and trustworthy leadership in every aspect of life. *Organizational Behavior Essentials You Always Wanted to Know* is a great tool and resource to have on any manager's bookshelf. Its reference to leadership skills and advice on how to manage effectively can help anyone coming into the role develop their practices. I recommend this book if you are learning the art of leadership, or just need reminders on the aspects of management.

– Annie Bahringer
Library Director, North Shore Library

What experts say about this book!

Organizational Behavior Essentials is a well-organized and insightful course or text designed to teach you how effective and forward-thinking organizations should be managed in today's modern and changing environment. Each chapter is structured to present a lesson relating to the chapter topic, followed by a chapter summary to reinforce the lesson, and finally, a "brief" quiz to ensure the reader has absorbed the lesson that has been presented. Human resources and talent development within the modern organization is the primary focus of this text with a concentration on the development of high-performance employees and teams. Organizational Behavior Essentials emphasizes the need to be inclusive and embrace diversity and cultural differences at all levels in the organization while highlighting the costs and risks incurred when organizations ignore diversity. Even the less human resources-oriented chapters on communications, power & politics, or decision-making & conflict still concentrate on the human impact that the subject has on the organization.

Organizational Behavior Essentials will make a valuable addition to a business library or a public library with a business collection.

– Tim Neale
Aurora Public Library

This page is intentionally left blank

Table of Contents

Section 1: Introduction

1 **What is Organizational Behavior? History, Theories, Global Perspectives**   **1**

1.1 The Changing Workplace   3
1.2 The Challenge of Increased Quality   4
1.3 Employee Motivation and Commitment   5
1.4 Global Organizational Behavior   7
1.5 Leadership Responsibilities   9
1.6 Training   10
1.7 Diversity and Inclusion   10
1.8 Globalization and Leadership   13
1.9 Global Culture and Communication   16
Quiz   18
Chapter Summary   22

Section 2: The Individual

2 **Understanding People at Work: Diversity and Individual Differences**   **25**

2.1 Inclusion Leadership   30
2.2 Workplace Diversity   31
2.3 Managing Differences   32
Quiz   34
Chapter Summary   38

3 Motivation and Reinforcement 39

3.1 Key Concepts of Reinforcement 41

3.2 Motivation 43

3.3 Expectancy Theory of Motivation 45

3.4 Performance Management and Motivation 46

Quiz 48

Chapter Summary 52

4 Perceptions, Decision-Making, and Problem Solving 55

4.1 Perceptions and Behavior 57

4.2 Problem Solving 59

4.3 Decision Making 61

4.4 Decision Making Framework 62

Quiz 64

Chapter Summary 68

5 Theories in Talent Development 71

5.1 Talent Development and Training 72

5.2 ADDIE - Analysis 76

5.3 ADDIE - Design 77

5.4 ADDIE - Development 79

5.5 ADDIE - Implementation and Evaluation 80

5.6 Kirkpatrick Model 81

5.7 Globalization of Training 84

Quiz 85

Chapter Summary 88

Section 3: The Group

6 Group Behavior, Teamwork and High-Performance Teams 89

6.1 Stage 1: Forming 90

6.2 Stage 2: Storming 90

6.3 Stage 3: Norming 91

6.4 Stage 4: Performing 91

6.5 Stage 5: Adjourning 92

6.6 Team Development 95

6.7 Cultural Differences 96

6.8 Qualities of High-Performing Teams 97

6.9 Talent Acquisition 98

6.10 Rewards and Motivation 99

6.11 Leadership and Communication 99

6.12 Empowering Teams 100

Quiz 101

Chapter Summary 105

7 High-Performance Job Designs 107

7.1 The Value of High-Performing Work Systems 109

7.2 High-Performance Work Systems and Employee Empowerment 110

7.3 Role of Human Resources in High-Performance Job Designs and Work Systems 111

7.4 Technology in High-Performance Organizations 112

7.5 Align Goals with Business Strategy 112

7.6 Performance Management in HPWS 113

7.7 Impact of High-Performance Work Systems 113

Quiz 115

Chapter Summary 119

8 **Information and Communication** **121**

8.1 Communication Within Organization 125

8.2 Groups and Teams 125

Quiz 129

Chapter Summary 132

9 **Power and Politics** **135**

9.1 Different Ways Organizations Use Power 137

9.2 Power at all Levels 139

9.3 Power and Leadership 140

Quiz 141

Chapter Summary 144

10 **Decision Making, Conflict, and Negotiation** **147**

10.1 Decision Making Leadership 150

10.2 Communication 151

10.3 Motivation and Accountability 152

10.4 Building Positive Relationships 152

Quiz 154

Chapter Summary 158

Section 4: Organizations

11 Basic Attributes of Organizations   **161**

11.1 Different Leadership Role and Skills   163

11.2 Organizational Global Culture   163

11.3 Organizational Environment and Motivation   165

11.4 Managing Workplace Stress   167

11.5 Leadership: Fundamentals and Emerging Perspectives   168

Quiz   170

Chapter Summary   174

12 Strategic Competency and Organizational Design   **177**

12.1 Technology Supports Technology   179

12.2 Organizational Design and Talent Pool   181

12.3 Cultivate Leadership   182

12.4 Elevate Training Initiatives   183

Quiz   185

Chapter Summary   189

13 High-Performance Organizational Cultures   **191**

13.1 Creating a High-Performance Culture   194

13.2 From Vision to Performance   195

13.3 Traits of High-Performance Work Teams   196

Quiz   198

Chapter Summary   202

14 Change 205

14.1 Change Management   206

14.2 Successful Change – What it Takes   209

14.3 Assessing Organizational Readiness and Adaptability to Change   212

Quiz   216

Chapter Summary   220

15 Human Resource Management Systems 223

15.1 HRMS Effectiveness and Efficiencies   227

15.2 Recruitment Tracking   229

15.3 Confidential Personnel Files   229

15.4 Payroll   229

15.5 Benefits Administration   230

15.6 Learning and Development   230

15.7 Performance Management   231

Quiz   232

Chapter Summary   235

16 Assessments Used in Organizational Behavior 237

16.1 Surveys and Questionnaires – Unveiling Organizational Insights   238

16.2 Personality, Behavioral, Emotional Intelligence, and Strengths Assessments   241

16.3 Team and Organizational Effectiveness Assessments   252

Quiz   257

Chapter Summary   261

Glossary 263

Bibliography 267

Preface

Organizational Behavior is the study of the complex inner workings of organizations. It is a macroscopic view of employees, teams, departments, divisions, and other parts of businesses, corporations, governments, and other groups. Organizational Behavior covers the relationships between individuals, between groups within an organization, and between an organization and the rest of the world. The world of work in this century is very different from what it was 15 years ago. Today's work environment is technological, innovative, and multicultural. Businesses encompass diverse global teams to fulfill their goals. In any organization or its respective divisions, there is more prominent diversity in terms of demographic characteristics, interests, and cultures than in past decades.

Mental and physical abilities remain important attributes for predicting job success, personality, and interpersonal skills. Organizational behavior is the study of individual and group performance and activity within an organization. The study incorporates parts dedicated to job performance: amplifying job fulfillment, advancing innovation, and inspiring leadership.

How to use this book?

1. This book can be used as a guide or reference to understand the role of Organizational Behavior within an organization as well as the role of Human Resources or OD practitioners in leading organizational change initiatives.

2. The book should be approached with an open mind regarding the possibilities and the paths to which it could lead. This is the case because Organizational Behavior is an evolving discipline with new research being added consistently, and the impact of technology being a driving force behind organizational change.

3. It should be read as a general introduction to the subject. Each section itself could be its own book. Should a particular section or chapter inspire the reader, (s)he should follow up by researching that specific area of interest.

4. For practitioners, the book should also serve as a sounding board or reality check. Over time, one tends to start building comfort and prejudice in certain areas of the subject. The same might happen with Organizational Behavior, especially in the areas of which tools or models to use.

5. Recognize the bibliography as a comprehensive list of resources and tools to research and investigate further.

Who can benefit from this book?

This book can be useful for a cross-section of people:

1. For a management professional, it will provide a foundational understanding of Organizational Behavior with a comprehensive assessment of tools to be used for organizational development and change management initiatives within an organization.

2. For an OD or Human Resources professional, it should serve as a refresher on some of the core concepts and disciplines but it also offers deeper insights in terms of assessing an organization's readiness for change and evaluating individual, team, and organizational strengths.

3. For a business school professor, it will offer a comprehensive evaluation of Organizational Behavior to be used as a primary or supplemental read within their courses.

4. For students, it will introduce the topic of Organizational Behavior and its link to Organizational Development and Change Management, offering vocational awareness to pursue a career in the discipline and understand its critical role within organizations.

5. For business leaders, the book may create awareness and offer diagnostic tools to identify and evaluate potential strengths and shadows within their organizations through the facilitation of a comprehensive library of assessments, equipping them with the tools and insights to proactively lead organizational development and change management initiatives.

6. And, of course, anyone with a desire to learn more about the subject would benefit from this book as well.

This page is intentionally left blank

Chapter **1**

What is Organizational Behavior? History, Theories, Global Perspectives

Beginning in this chapter and continuing throughout this course, we will cover numerous examples of how companies from around the world meet the challenges of global competition. Organizational behavior helps to build enhanced workplace interactions and connections between workers. Organizations plan for success using either fundamental or innovative strategies. They set goals and build teams to meet those goals. They hire visionary leaders who can see beyond current market trends and plan for a successful future. They create a structure to efficiently plan, collaborate, communicate, solve problems, and meet customer demands. They navigate change while either steadfastly maintaining a certain course of action or by pivoting to gain an edge over their competition or shaping the market with bold action. Organizations are complex, unique, and varied. They have similarities and differences we will investigate.

What will be covered in this chapter

- The changing workplace

- The challenge of increased quality

- Characteristics of high-performance organizations including (high-performing teams, strategic planning, change readiness, knowledge skills and abilities, communication, high-performance leadership)

- Employee motivation and commitment

- Global organizational behavior

- Organizational behavior dimensions including (strategy and structure, obtaining management support, empowering and developing teams, seizing opportunities, remaining customer focused, influencing corporate culture, shared purpose and vision, coaching people, shaping the environment, agile leadership, leading through change, promoting the company's vision)

- Leadership responsibilities

- Communication Impacts on Organizational Culture including (strategic alignment with employees, leadership behaviors to build the system, measuring performance through success with customers, continuous process improvement)

- Training and development

- Diversity and inclusion
- Globalization and leadership
- Global culture and communication

1.1 The Changing Workplace

Technological disruptions have hindered the work environments in numerous ways. They can be visually perceived in the augmented utilization of automation, robotics, and expert systems such as Human Capital Management (HCM), Enterprise Resource Planning (ERP), and computer-integrated manufacturing systems, which altered the way many products are manufactured today. Such changes influence not only production proficiency and product excellence but also the nature of jobs. Many businesses are replacing front-line supervisors with self-managing work teams who assume accountability for overall department operation as well as production planning, quality control, and even performance appraisals.

These constant innovative and technological changes require business leaders to implement workplace transformations to adapt these technological disruptions while still developing their workforce. Managers can respond to the technological imperative while preserving and improving the human resources of the company. In terms of corporate resilience, striving to become more efficient is perhaps the biggest challenge for management Greater competition requires careful consideration of people, groups, and whole organizational structures.

1.2 The Challenge of Increased Quality

To stay ahead of competitive advantage and establish market competitiveness and other correlated factors such as cost-efficient operational efficiency, production and manufacturing efficiency, budget controls, learning and development investments. Total Quality Management is responsible for enhanced quality control of products and services that are constantly requested by customers. Total Quality Management is defined as the high-level efforts to monitor and improve quality of product and processes within a firm. As an example, automotive giant BMW is recognized for its high standards, quality, and service. Therefore, the competitive advantage for BMW is the superiority of its luxury cars.

Principally, if organizations want to stay ahead of their competition, they must be dedicated to high quality products for their customers. One of the biggest challenges an organization faces is to encourage their employees to create a superior quality of products and services.

Figure 1.1 Characteristics of a high-performance organization

1.3 Employee Motivation and Commitment

Adversarial relationships between leadership and employees that organizations accepted in the past are a major hurdle in the pursuit of industrial competitiveness. Organizations face situations where the average employee clearly sees no reason to increase output or improve the quality of current outputs whether an organization is unionized or not. The company's reward system frequently restricts performance, rather than improving it. At other times, rewards encourage employees to increase quantity at the expense of quality. Furthermore, North American organizations often view their workforce as a variable expense and often cut jobs over short term operational or budget gains. As a result, the organization is lacking employee commitment. Rates of turnover and absenteeism are often unreasonably high, further eroding the efficiency and effectiveness of the performance.

If businesses are to succeed in an increasingly turbulent environment, managers need to find better ways to create and motivate employees. The workforce of an organization is often its largest asset and failing to appropriately manage it results in a poor return on the organization's investment.

In the business world, organizations that manage the global complexity and interrelationships will accomplish high levels of organizational efficiency and competitive advantage compared to other organizations. Many global organizations are currently wrestling to meet the quality demands of the customers and as a result, companies are becoming more and more dynamic and competitive to adapt new mechanisms, tools to make their organizations more agile and flexible. This approach is helping organizations to strengthen economic initiatives globally. However, to achieve this effectiveness and flexibility within the organizations many companies are moving toward shared service models for functions such as product management, human resources, finance, supply chain, etc. These functions are centralized and serving different business units of the organizations. To align with the shared service models, the organizations employ Human resource business partners, finance business partners, product manager business partners in every business unit that interact with shared functions and yet support sales leaders of their respective business units.

Global organizations and the international economy have been around for decades; however, today's global and economic business activities pose different challenges for organizations. Developing global strategies and managing global and diverse cultures is the new norm for the managers. Business leaders are expected to have a motivational approach; a total rewards system that ties into employee growth, organizational design is customized for different work groups. Innovative approaches are required to serve the global market as opposed to the traditional markets.

1.4 Global Organizational Behavior

Business leaders of global companies must have local sensitivity with global knowledge and strategic skills to understand and serve local markets with global flavor. Few examples of global companies with local presence like McDonalds for U.S. Customers serve different flavors, while McDonalds in India and China have different local offerings, Proctor and Gamble's detergent is customized for European markets due to the different make of the washing machines. These are just some of the examples of organizations serving local markets with global presence.

This global dynamic adds more complexity to the culture of the organizations. Companies need to implement and manage cross-culture, cross-border groups. The need for global networks, systems, processes, compliance adds to the culture's complexity. Companies should not ignore the cultural differences while developing a cross-cultural environment. Managers must learn to manage individual differences while organizing functions, business units, skills/tasks, etc. Communication skills are a key factor in globalization. Managers with global teams will need to be able to communicate with diverse culture teams, multilingual skills will be a plus.

Global organizations have many complexities to work around from people, structure, processes, etc. However, there are some best practices that can mitigate some of the risks.

Figure 1.2   Organizational Behavior Dimensions in Organizations

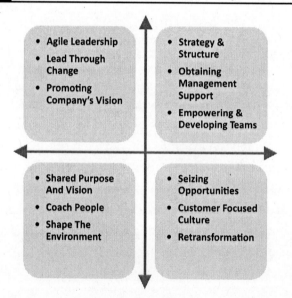

1.5 Leadership Responsibilities

The leadership team has the highest responsibilities in a high-performing organization. It is not just about getting work done within the team; on the contrary, the role is about the increasing demand to get innovative when managing remote teams with diverse cultures globally. The traditional style of leadership is less effective with the virtual organizations worldwide. While there are still full-time and regular employees in organizations, the companies are also reaching out to contractors and consultants for special projects. While technology is helping solve many operational issues, the managers are still struggling to find a common approach that works with different employee groups they work with.

Leading organizations are becoming tougher than ever. On one side, we have many energetic, enthusiastic, capable workforces who are in different parts of the world with different time zones – while on the other hand, we have traditional managers who are yet to learn and apply new ideas to manage people. Fundamentally, the organization is composed of people and this is the basic reason why managers must have great knowledge on employee behaviors and underlying emotions to produce positive business results.

1.6 Training

Core elements of the organizational behavior are people, structure, technology and environment. Not only do managers need to hone their communication skills in a global environment, but there are some crucial factors of organizational behavior that must be considered. People are the most intrinsic element of an organizational social system. Companies are required to be highly innovative in their total reward systems due to the increased competitiveness across the job market. Global organizations like IBM, PricewaterhouseCoopers (PwC), etc., are already using virtual cross functional teams across their different functions. With the remote teams, challenge comes to maintain trust and build relationships among each other. Managing cross-functional teams requires training for the managers to educate them on managing these types of employee groups. The training should also focus on employees understanding their own cultural beliefs, different communication styles including verbal and non-verbal, different personalities, etc.

1.7 Diversity and Inclusion

One of the most important benefits of having a diverse workforce is the ability for businesses to make quality decisions. In a diverse environment, people and teams usually have different perspectives and opinions coming from different cultures and backgrounds. Particularly in diverse teams, people are more willing to consider alternate views and they tend to think outside the box while making decisions. An organization with a diverse workforce is more likely to create products and solutions that appeal to different ethnic, diverse, and broad customer base. PepsiCo was able to grow 8% revenue due to diverse marketing efforts back in 2004. They also increased the women and ethnic minority groups in management and other levels within the organization. Similarly, Harley-Davidson is pursuing diversification marketing efforts to reach a different customer base. To promote these efforts, the company is promoting diversity and inclusion at all levels in order to stay competitive.

The new diversity mantra, in a global economy is more complicated than ever and is no longer about how many people we have in the teams, rather it is about how many diverse people we have in a team to reach higher quality decisions. Teams with the most diversity understand the needs of their client groups and customers better and companies earn the trust of their customers faster and better. Additionally, when diverse employees are treated equally and fairly, they tend to be motivated and satisfied. Whereas if the workforce is not treated fairly in a diverse organization, the company loses the credibility it had within the workforce.

Organizations that do a better job at increasing the diversity of their employees and customers see more rewards on the stock market and gain the trust of the investors. Investors can judge a company's long-term growth based on their diversity efforts. Companies that perform in the top 10 financially are more diverse (Inclusion 2020). The other benefit the organization has with the increased diversity efforts is the low litigation expenses. Companies with poor diversity efforts have high expenses on lawsuits. When companies do not pay attention to the EEOC and violate the laws, employees may file a complaint with the EEOC. And the EEOC will investigate the complaint and act as a mediator with the people and the company. If they do not reach the settlement, the EEOC will file the lawsuit against the company. Nevertheless, of the outcome, these lawsuits are extremely expensive and come at the cost of bad branding for the organization. For example, Coca-Cola was faced with a lawsuit for racial discrimination resulting in a $192 million settlement. As a result of these efforts, companies that manage their diversity efforts effectively tend to outperform their competition.

The diversity efforts come with challenges, such as to manage creative solutions with a diverse workforce toward fair and equal treatment. Many times, there is a similarity phenomenon within the organization recruitment efforts in hiring people who are "similar to us," and this may be potentially an unfair treatment based on the demographic traits. The similarity phenomenon may also affect employees in their daily work environment. For example, a woman in a similar position to her male coworker does not get invited to business leaders meeting – whereas a male coworker gets regular invitations to these meetings, after-hours dinners, etc., which may be a sign of sexual discrimination. The other challenge of diversity efforts is often the perception and stereotypes it creates among the different workgroups. The problem is the stereotype that the organization or teams often make decisions about a particular person or ethnic group with underlying assumptions. Due to this, it may often lead to unfair treatment and inaccurate decision making leading to bad branding and a negative impact on revenue in the long run.

1.8 Globalization and Leadership

Leadership is basically the act of influencing others. This is especially true for today's world where global economies are becoming more interconnected. Organizations can demonstrate leadership via formal and informal leadership approaches. This is one of the biggest challenges for organizations to train future leaders and improve their leadership capabilities. When organizations fail to train their leadership team effectively, many issues arise in the organization including communication gaps, change management, discrimination, etc. As organizations work persistently to become more accustomed to thinking in short-term gains with an eye on long-term gains, management can deal with the global economic situations and implement positive results within the organization. As a benefit, it is significant to recognize how leadership can be used to lead in a globalized environment. There are different types of the leaders: tasks-oriented leaders and people-oriented leaders. While task-oriented leaders are able to put together the structure and processes within the organization; people-oriented leaders are able to help the organizations by demonstrating that people-related compassionate behaviors tend to prevail. Additionally, there are many other leadership styles that benefit different situations within the organizations as highlighted in the path-goal theory of 1971. This theory is used by the leaders to create motivated high-performing teams that support global organizations and the economic health of the world.

1.8.1 Supportive Leaders

They provide emotional support to their teams. Employees are treated well, and managers tend to care about the employee's well-being. Supportive leaders encourage their team members to go the extra mile while considering their stress levels and capabilities to perform a task.

1.8.2 Directive Leaders

Directive leaders clarify the expectations of their team and give clear directions to perform a task. They set the schedules, clarify roles and expectations, and make sure that employees are aware of their schedules and what is expected of them on any given day. However, directive leadership is less effective with high-skilled people.

1.8.3 Participative Leaders

Participative leaders ensure that employees are involved in every phase of the decision-making process. This is the most effective leadership style with high-performing employees. High-performing employees with high skills and job-specific knowledge often require autonomy to complete the tasks and participative leadership styles support this.

1.8.4 High-achievement Leaders

This type of leadership style motivates and encourages teams to reach their full potential. Leaders challenge the teams to focus on business results while reaching their full potential and learning the skills of the future. Supporting high-performing employees with high ability and high levels of motivation reaching job satisfaction is one of the key outcomes of this type of leadership.

Fast growing global economies are affecting global organizations in different areas on how these organizations are interconnected with people, political and social environments. Innovation in technology is driving the way businesses are managed today with the quickly changing organizational cultures. The products and services are traded across borders and corporations must be ready to understand and manage cross-border implications with the impact of globalization. This is forcing organizational leaders at all levels to embrace the culture differences and ensure that the organization is operating at the highest levels of efficiency.

Global organizational structures and volatile economic frameworks continue to amplify their communication measures between diverse cultures. While innovations have driven organizations to contribute to a universal business, global leaders require the aptitude and experience essential to lead well in a globalized environment. Transformational leadership is recognized as the leadership style most capable of working cross-culturally to improve the motivation and performance, and to drive much-needed change in the global setting.

1.9 Global Culture and Communication

Virtual, remote work setting is the new norm in a global organization. The leaders have teams that are managed cross-country and cross-functionally. This virtual communication requires innovations in managing teams from different countries, learning their cultures and collaborating to achieve business bottom line results, specifically how the communication works among the group members especially those who come from diverse backgrounds and sometimes lack social cues. Managing cultural differences and cross-cultural clashes is one of the key components for leadership in the current dynamic and volatile market. Cross-cultural communication competence is the most important component of a leader's aptitude to solve any performance challenges.

Figure 1.3   Communication Impacts on Organizational Culture

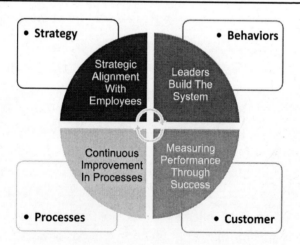

With the global onset, the expat managers or leaders have a higher responsibility of learning strong technical skills and good language skills with specific country knowledge. Often the first-time expatriate manager will receive a culture shock when they visit a new country. Culture shock is defined as the frustration and confusion that results when faced with strange and unfamiliar cues of how to do things. The successful expatriate will cope effectively with such situations. This is where the organizations can support their new managers to overcome some of these challenges. Companies can invest in the culture training for these expatriate managers and employees to ensure success of the incoming employee from another part of the world. Intercultural training has a positive impact on new employees in the country and provides a sense of positive security. The expatriate training must cover a few key topics such as language skills, nature and culture orientation, an overview of the employment laws of that respective country, personal and family orientation, and career planning as part of the planning for departure. During the overseas assignment, Human Resources should focus on additional training for this employee in a new country that potentially can include local mentoring, stress training, business issues, etc. Training that prepares an employee includes critical activities that can help prepare the expatriate for overseas assignments.

Quiz

1. Increasing technological complexity is _____.

  a. destroying the workplace

  b. changing the workplace

  c. making companies bigger

  d. hurting manufacturing companies

2. _____ is an important part of an organization.

  a. lobby size

  b. a large parking structure

  c. quality assurance

  d. number of offices

3. Simply offering bonuses for speed tends to encourage employees to _____.

  a. do a good job

  b. talk to coworkers

  c. cut corners

  d. take more breaks

4. Simply offering bonuses for quality tends to encourage employees to _____.

   a. take their time

   b. increase their speed

   c. argue with managers

   d. make no change in their behavior

5. What are two shared services that organizations can outsource to save time and money?

   a. Maintenance and supply chain

   b. Human resources and payroll

   c. Leadership and mentoring

   d. Diversity and inclusion

6. Companies are forced to navigate _____ relationships between organizations.

   a. easy

   b. strict

   c. uncomplicated

   d. complex

7. **Although most employees are _____, full-time workers, organizations increasingly use contract labor for temporary projects.**

   a. well-paid

   b. permanent

   c. underpaid

   d. temporary

8. **The EEOC is most often involved in which types of lawsuits?**

   a. Slip and fall

   b. Concussion

   c. Intellectual property

   d. Wrongful termination and harassment

9. **Different leadership styles _____.**

   a. are all the same

   b. do not affect employee behavior

   c. have strengths and weaknesses

   d. not understood at all

10. _____ are replacing traditional face-to-face meetings.

    a. work lunches

    b. virtual communications

    c. powerpoint presentations

    d. boardroom meetings

Answers	1 – b	2 – c	3 – c	4 – a	5 – b
	6 – d	7 – b	8 – d	9 – c	10 – b

Chapter Summary

Increasing technological complexity is changing the workplace. Business leaders need to adapt to these changes in technology and help their organizations to adapt as well. Quality assurance is an important part of an organization. Consumers buy the product with the best value, which is a combination of cost and quality. The workforce is the organization's greatest asset. Motivating employees is increasingly nuanced. Simply offering bonuses for speed creates incentives to cut corners. Offering bonuses for quality encourages employees to spend more time, which can sometimes be inefficient. Employees are motivated by more than money, including a sense of belonging and an understanding of how individual efforts benefit the organization and its customers. Business leaders are moving toward more complete rewards systems tied into employee growth. Companies are increasingly forced to navigate complex relationships between organizations. One way they are trying to keep up is through shared services for human resources, payroll, supply chain, etc. By outsourcing these tasks, an organization is able to spend more time and attention on endeavors specific to the organization above all others. Leaders of global companies must be responsive to local market demands. Just because it works in one country does not mean it will work everywhere. Organizations with departments in different countries must be aware of cross-cultural communications requirements when building teams and interdepartmental dependencies. Although most employees are permanent, full-time workers, organizations are increasingly using contract labor and consultants to supplement the workforce for temporary initiatives. Training in a global organization should include learning to understand the behaviors and ideals of others. Having a diverse workforce increases the quality of decisions because varied perspectives increase the likelihood of considering all key factors.

Increased focus on diversity also helps avoid lawsuits that could be filed with the Equal Opportunity Employment Commission (EEOC) on the basis of wrongful termination or harassment. Diversity includes the normal challenges of interpersonal conflict based on misunderstanding each other. Management is responsible for creating an environment conducive to healthy communication and effective teamwork. Different leadership styles have strengths and weaknesses. Not everyone responds to the same style of leadership so leaders need to be willing to modify their approach for maximum effectiveness. Virtual communication methods are replacing traditional face-to-face meetings. Global organizations need to be aware of potential struggles arising from misunderstood cues. Managers who visit a new country for the first time should be briefed before they leave so they do not experience culture shock and potentially represent the company in a negative way.

This page is intentionally left blank

Chapter **2**

Understanding People at Work: Diversity and Individual Differences

Work is similar to family because who we work with is usually out of our control like our immediate family. Adults can usually choose who they interact with to some degree by walking away from unpleasant, harmful, or dangerous situations and places. We spend most of our waking hours at work with coworkers and we have to make the best of it. It helps to remember individual differences drive most behavioral differences and understanding this simple fact can help keep things in perspective.

What will be covered in this chapter

- Different dimensions of diversity including (religion, culture, sexual orientation, geographic origin, social class, race, ethnicity, education, experience, nationality, language, cognitive ability,

- Inclusion leadership

- Workplace diversity

- Managing differences

- Diversity and inclusion framework including (executive sponsorship and buy-in, identifying and analyzing needs, strategy map for diversity and inclusion, developing new initiatives, continuous monitoring and improvement)

In the previous chapter, we touched on diversity and inclusion. Here we can further explore the topic to understand how diversity and individual differences come together at a workplace. The leadership team plays an especially important role in forming a diverse organization. Individual differences play a vital role in organizations. People bring their personalities, emotions, perceptions, and physical and mental abilities to a workplace. While people bring many traits to the workplaces, every organization is unique with its culture, vision, and goals and therefore to survive the economic global environment with a high-performance culture, these leaders are under high pressure for diversity and inclusion efforts.

When a new hire joins the organization, they take time to observe and learn the culture of the organization while bringing their perceptions to work. Recruitment efforts of the organizations usually focus on person-organization fit and person-position fit. Jim Collins, in his book Good to Great, used the example of the organization as a bus. First get the right people on the bus, and then get the people in the right seats. The first step is where a person is evaluated against the organizational culture, personal values, and goals. The next step is where the applicant is evaluated against the position expectations, skills, abilities, and deliverables. In this case, applicants with out of the box thinking, creative ideas and good ability to manage change will succeed. Proactive individuals with risk-taking abilities will prevail in the job market.

Inclusion is being included or including others' values and perspective in workplaces. Valuing, respecting, and engaging our workforces that are coming from diverse cultures are an important key factor for business leaders to thrive in global context. As a diverse business leader, a cross-functional approach is critical to success of the organization. The ability to understand and manage the psychological aspect of the group dynamics helps in effective implementing and leading the key elements of the corporate strategy.

Apple proudly declares on its website, "At Apple, we're not all the same. And that's our greatest strength. We draw on the differences in who we are, what we've experienced, and how we think. Because to create products that serve everyone, we believe in including everyone" (Apple, 2020). The topic of diversity and inclusion comes up more than ever as these are the most increasingly recognized in the meeting with the leaders. However, even though these topics may be discussed in board meetings, they may not necessarily have reached the mid-level management and staff level employees. Organizations understand the value of a diverse workforce, but unless these topics are included in all the functions such as recruitment, sales, marketing & branding, etc., they may not reach the employees and customers. Therefore, if only a few of the components of social identity of employees are included by the organization it may still make them feel excluded despite the efforts. These attitudes may influence the underlying beliefs and emotions of the employees, in turn leading to low motivation, performance issues, low morale and employee engagement, etc., ultimately impacting the profitability and growth of the organization.

It is critical for organizations to understand the impact of diversity and inclusion on individual employees, groups of individuals, teams, and overall organization. Typically, the organization's performance and employee engagement success are determined by the employee engagement surveys to determine if an organization has an inclusive environment that makes employees feel welcome.

Excellence in Diversity and Inclusion efforts is one of the toughest challenges for an organization, mainly because it is an extremely broad term. For many, diversity is about ethnic or racial differences, different age groups, sexual orientation, marital status, etc. However, diversity is not only limited to these areas but in much more than that. It can be interpreted in different ways in different organizations based on the culture of the company. Workplace diversity has become a branding tool in which companies promote the diversity not only internally but also externally with their customers, partners, vendors, and community. Fortune 500 and global organizations hire diverse workforces with different ethnic backgrounds, skills, race, gender, etc., to ensure they have diverse teams. This also puts pressure on supervisors to learn to manage different types of teams evenly and equitably. The financial performance of the organizations improves with the most diversified workforce and cultures (Levine, 2020). Growth predictions and sustainability of the organization is also improved with the diverse culture across the organization. Inclusion requires a deeper understanding and more focus from business leaders. This requires a fundamental change within the organizational structures, policies, processes, leadership style, and culture dynamics of the business. Overall, diversity and inclusion change all the levels within the organization, and the way individuals and teams interact with each other. Inclusion requires leadership and employees to collaborate with a positive attitude and behaviors toward the job and the organization.

Figure 2.1	Different Dimensions of Diversity

Thinking Ability · Religion · Culture · Language · Sexual Orientation · Nationality · **Diversity** · Geographic Origin · Experience · Family Status · Education · Ethnicity · Race

2.1 Inclusion Leadership

Diversity and inclusion have gained an advantage in the global context. Organizations are functioning more and more in a global environment and serving global customers, so this topic has gained attention with business leaders and has become a key priority to grow and sustain an organization. Diverse customer segments, market penetration and tough talent acquisition challenges demand the need for inclusion leadership. There are a few key attributes of an inclusive leader that demonstrate the ability of embracing individual differences and leveraging the differences for business competitiveness.

Market Diversification

In this volatile ever-changing market, demand is shifting to new markets. Organizations are trying to compete in the new emerging markets; thus, they are required to not only embrace the culture and differences of the new market but also train their workforces to support these new market demands. Similarly, customer demands are changing. Customers are increasingly becoming more aware about the alternate product and services options, which puts the organizations in a tough spot to be able to support diverse customer demands from sales and marketing perspectives.

Technological Diversification

Technology is changing at a very rapid pace, faster than many companies could adapt. This is creating a challenging situation for companies to change their operations and processes at a rapid pace while serving customers' demands. Digital transformations across organizations are shaping up to sustain in the high-tech world. Not only is technology disrupting business value chains, but also there is a need for rapid innovation that supports market diversification.

Talent Diversification

With the diversity of market, customers, and technology, it is important to look at one of the highest cost centers of the organizations that need development. To meet rapidly changing customer demands and work with technological advancements, we need to be able to develop our talents for today but focused on the future. Shifts in baby boomers retiring while millennials are entering the job market require significant shifts from employers to transition the new generation while not isolating the older generation. Not only the shifts in age profiles but also in education, global mobility, and work-life balance expectations from employees must be considered and incorporated in organizations diversity and inclusion initiatives.

2.2 Workplace Diversity

For more than two decades, this topic has gained popularity among employers and employees of global organizations. Talent acquisition teams have various strategies to attract diversified talents. However, business leaders often struggle with understanding different perspectives in terms of globalization, unionization, and culture. There are many psychological factors as well that need to be considered such as race, ethnicity, sexual orientation, age, education, religion, disability, perceptions, and many others. Diversity management must be all-inclusive; that includes everyone in an organization with a goal to maximize diversity to achieve all organizational as well as individual goals. Effectively managing diversity and inclusion is more of enabling and empowering employees. Diversity and inclusion topics are not only cultural but also must be addressed in organizational policies, processes, training, and adapting to new strategies to recruit, retain, and engage the workforce to mirror the markets. One of the best business cases for diversity and inclusion is, "Wal-Mart - Think globally and serve locally." According to Wal-Mart, they use the diversity and inclusion efforts to attract, recruit, retain and engage workforces that foster diverse culture, according to a Wal-Mart 2015 Diversity report.

2.3 Managing Differences

Approaching and managing diversity and inclusion in the workplace often consists of some key characteristics like:

- Establishing, identifying, and analyzing the needs of the diverse employee workgroups - organizations should be proactive in identifying the needs of their workgroups, and analyzing the culture of the business. Educating employees and managers about embracing the differences of coworkers, culture, customers, partners, etc.

- Designing the diversity strategy for an organization - designing the framework of the diversity initiatives by leveraging the best practices of research and other organizations - will help in formulating the program that is best suited to a particular organization.

- Developing new diversity initiatives addressing different groups - Different workgroups require different motivation and it is important for business leaders and human resource professionals to understand the needs of each diverse workgroup and develop new initiatives keeping different workgroups in mind. Making sure there is fair and equitable treatment for different workgroups.

- Continuous monitoring, evaluating, and improving the entire diversity and inclusion process and strategy - it is not only important to design and develop the diversity program but also important to continuously monitor and evaluate the program from time to time to ensure that the program is working well and improve as needed.

Figure 2.2   Diversity and Inclusion Framework

Step 1: Executive Sponsorship & Buy-In

Step 3: Strategy Map for Diversity & Inclusion

Step 5: Continuous Monitoring & Improvement

Step 2: Identifying & Analyzing Needs

Step 4: Developing New Initiatives

Many high-performance organizations understand this as an important topic. They have strategic goals and continuously monitor all HR systems and processes, adapt to the changing market demands, and recruit and retain diverse workgroups to serve and sustain customers in the global context.

Quiz

---

1. **Why is it important for organizations to fully understand Diversity includes differences such as _____.**

   a. race or ethnicity

   b. sex

   c. religion

   d. all of the above

2. **Companies are under greater pressure to increase diversity _____.**

   a. above everything else

   b. in one category only

   c. to try to match the diversity of the surrounding community

   d. because the government forces it

3. **New employees are often hired based on two types of qualifications: whether they are a right fit for _____ and whether they are a right fit for _____.**

   a. sales, marketing

   b. leadership, obedience

   c. the organization, a specific job opening

   d. intelligence, personality

4. Inclusion involves _____ regarding one's personality, perspectives, skills, etc.

   a. strict scrutiny

   b. aloofness

   c. speculation

   d. being included and including others

5. How do organizations think about diversity?

   a. All organizations view diversity exactly the same

   b. Organizations are unaware of diversity

   c. All organizations view diversity differently

   d. Organizations only worry about diversity

6. For companies to maximize diversity, they must focus on _____ including recruitment, sales, marketing, and branding.

   a. as many methods as possible

   b. as few methods as possible

   c. sales figures

   d. training

7. **Even if diversity and inclusion are discussed _____, it may not be well understood or implemented by mid-level management or front-line employees.**

   a. on the news

   b. in the break room

   c. in the boardroom

   d. in business classes

8. **The treatment of different employees and workgroups should be _____ and _____.**

   a. just, deserving

   b. happy, healthy

   c. fair, equitable

   d. stern, strict

9. **Many organizations put considerable effort into _____ and _____ because they value the results.**

   a. training, break rooms

   b. diversity, inclusion

   c. parking lots, lobbies

   d. travel, expenses

10. The financial performance of the organizations improves with the most diversified workforce and cultures.

a. True

b. False

c. Only in small organizations

d. Only in large organizations

Answers	1 – d	2 – c	3 – c	4 – d	5 – c
	6 – a	7 – c	8 –c	9 – b	10 – a

Chapter Summary

Diversity covers individual differences in background, personality, race/ethnicity, sex, gender, orientation, religion, etc. Companies are under greater pressure to improve diversity especially if the demographics within the company do not match the demographics of the surrounding area. Organizations generally want to appear fair and welcoming so they often pay particular attention to diversity and inclusion. New employees were often hired based on two types of qualifications: whether they are a right fit for the organization and whether they are a right fit for a specific job opening. One example is to get the right people on the bus and then put the people in the right seats. Inclusion involves being included and including others regarding one's personality, perspectives, skills, etc. Even if diversity and inclusion are discussed in board room meetings, it may not be well understood or implemented by mid-level management or front-line employees. Different organizations think of diversity differently. For companies to maximize diversity, they must focus on as many methods as possible, including recruitment, sales, marketing and branding. Companies strive to penetrate new markets, which means they need to understand the diverse needs of the customers in that market. Treatment of different employees and workgroups should be fair and equitable. Many organizations put considerable effort into diversity and inclusion because they value the results.

Chapter 3

Motivation and Reinforcement

This chapter discusses how organizations use motivation and reinforcement to persuade employees to act in certain ways. This is usually done for the good of the company, the customer, or the employee. There are many ways to inspire or threaten employees and most organizations try to motivate workers as nicely as possible. Organizations generally try not to threaten employees, but an example of a necessary threat is telling an employee this is the last warning before termination due to extremely unacceptable behavior that harms fellow employees, hurts the company's profit, reputation, business partners, or customers. Beyond ethical motivation and reinforcement or unethical methods of harmful manipulation, there are many subtle ways to alter behavior intentionally and unintentionally.

| What will be covered in this chapter |

- Key concepts of reinforcement

- Motivation

- Expectancy theory of motivation

- Performance management and motivation

Every employee's performance is extremely important in an organization. There are many motivation theories out there but one of the most common methods used is positive reinforcement in which employees' behavior is strengthened or improved based on the consequences. The idea is to understand and analyze the impact of positive reinforcement on the performance of employees by the way of extrinsic and intrinsic rewards. Some of the extrinsic rewards consist of salary, bonus, benefit plans, etc., and the intrinsic rewards are motivation, encouragement, or autonomy to make decisions, etc. When managers apply positive reinforcement by motivating or empowering team members, desired results are achieved that impacts the bottom line of the organization and also negative behaviors of employees are eliminated improving the culture overall. Both financial and non-financial rewards have a positive impact on the employee improving efficiency and effectiveness of the performance.

Positive reinforcement is a technique that is used for the past many years to elicit, strengthen, and reward new behaviors instead of eliminating benefits or rewards. Positive reinforcement is about providing intrinsic and extrinsic incentives to motivate employees instead of punishing them for negative behaviors. This approach can go the extra mile in increasing employee motivation and overall public image of the organization. It is prudent for an organization to motivate their workforce in a positive manner and ensure that the reinforcement is impacting performance in a positive and effective way.

Every employee's contribution is important in an organization. A way to motivate employees is through Skinner's reinforcement theory; one of the most common approaches used is where one's behavior is strengthened by using different positive reinforcement strategies that impacts the organizations. Over the years, managers are always concerned about their team's performance and motivation. They have been using different strategies to improve and enhance the performance of their teams. Positive reinforcement theories have affected organizations overall for many years. When a manager praises the employee, it encourages the employee in a positive way to do more than the minimum requirement in any given task. Similarly, when a manager punishes an employee, it negatively impacts the employee who loses the motivation or morale to work for any given task.

3.1 Key Concepts of Reinforcement

Reinforcement theory is divided into positive and negative reinforcement. Both positive and negative theories both impact job performance. However, with positive reinforcement, when managers communicate clearly and provide regular feedback to their team, it gives a sense of security and commitment for employees to go above and beyond on their performance. Effective organizations promote values and vision and employees who believe in the organization's vision are glad to positively impact the work culture. When employees are treated fairly and equally, they are more likely to be motivated and perform better.

Positive reinforcement is when the employees feel encouraged to perform better within an organization. Every employee's performance is critical for a company. Positive reinforcements for employees are things like salary, bonus, fringe benefits, and other internal rewards such as praise, encouragement, and empowerment.

Negative reinforcement is when the negative situation is stopped if the desired behavior is performed. For example, if the company is moving to a new office and employees are reluctant to move there, this is a potentially negative situation. However, the company decides to let the top performers choose whether they would like to move to the new office. In this case, the top performers will keep performing better to avoid moving. Employees will continue to perform at their best to avoid any negative consequences.

The theory of reinforcement is when the positive reinforcement behavior is practiced over a period of time. For organizations, it is important to ensure desired behavior from the employees and avoid conflicts. Usually, managers will encourage or discourage several things including organizational cultures, working in silos, leadership styles, etc.

Positive punishment is when a manager imposes a negative consequence to reduce the undesirable behavior. Negative punishment is a penalty for undesirable behavior, such as taking away an employee's optional position as the chair of a committee.

This is usually used as a last resort to rectify negative behavior and improve employee behavior. For example, employees regularly arriving late to work may have their pay docked. This will reduce their tendency to be late at work.

Extinction is meant to stop the negative behavior. When managers try to extinguish the desired behavior may be because it is no longer needed. For example, the organization decided to pay 20% extra to hourly production workers to volunteer for extra work during the Coronavirus shutdown. Organization used extra bonus pay as the positive reinforcement. However, things went back normal and managers stopped paying 20% for hourly workers. Their learned behavior (volunteering for extra work) is extinguished. This is usually an unintended consequence of temporary rewards, bonuses, and perks.

3.2 Motivation

Organizations are constantly trying to achieve sustained high-performance. High-performance organizations are focused on improving performance through culture and people. Therefore, high-performance culture is developed by high commitment and high involvement from management leadership. The goal of a high-performance organization is to create a climate where employees are motivated by positive reinforcement and achieve the highest levels of performance. Motivation is nothing but an internally generated drive for a person to accomplish a goal. Employees with high motivation are goal oriented and achievement focused. Motivated employees are more productive and have a positive attitude which improves the overall culture of the organization. There are several theories of motivation that are successful and used by the organizations including, but not limited to, hierarchy of needs theory, two-factor theory of expectancy theory, etc.

There are two main theories of motivation: extrinsic and intrinsic. Extrinsic motivation comes from external factors such as a bonus, pay raise or any other form of reward. Intrinsic motivation comes from within. It is a satisfaction from within, from a job well done or an accomplishment or achieving the desired level of outcome. According to Maslow's hierarchy of needs, people have different types of needs and the motivational factors are different as well. The needs are categorized as Physiological, Safety, Social, Esteem and Self-Actualization. Physiological needs are the needs most basic to our physiology— our body—such as food, water, and air. Safety needs are defined as the financial stability, freedom, or safe living environment. Social needs are met through rewarding time spent with family and friends. Esteem needs are met through self-respect and social status. Self-actualization needs are met when one reaches the ultimate life goal or reaches one's full potential. There are key considerations of Maslow's needs - the basic needs must be met before reaching higher level needs.

Figure 3.1

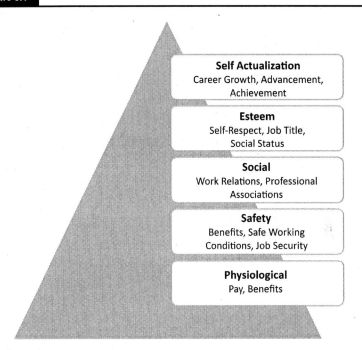

3.3 Expectancy Theory of Motivation

Expectancy theory of motivation focuses on employees who will be motivated by a belief in their ability to reach a goal while also expecting they will be rewarded for reaching the goal. Organizations set up reward structures to attract and retain key employees. If companies want the employee to give their highest performance, they must be able to put clear reward structures in place with SMART goals and regular evaluations. Employees who understand the clear goals will put forward their efforts to achieve those targets and rewards. Employees need to know the necessary actions to put forward in accomplishing a goal. Employees usually

base their level of efforts on their manager's response in team
meetings, annual evaluations, and feedback. This may include
encouraging feedback, or praise in front of colleagues, bonuses, or
appraisal letters.

3.4 Performance Management and Motivation

Performance management in organizations focus on improving
its organizational effectiveness by motivating employees to
accomplish the mission and goals of the companies. Companies
continuously monitor employee performance, developing them
to perform and reward good performance. In this globalization
environment, organizations are becoming competitive and
employees are becoming more skilled. Companies may be able to
survive with average employees, but high performer employees
will be able to support business goals at a greater height. In this
tight labor market, it is extremely important for organizations to
retain good employees and use different motivational strategies
to improve corporate culture. Improving productivity has been
a key challenge for the organizations. Employee engagement and
motivation of employees is a serious issue for many organizations.
Motivation increases organizational productivity; it is particularly
important for managers and leaders to understand the levels
of motivation of employees, why they behave differently at the
workplace, and how to positively reinforce the desired behavior.
The goal of every leader is to ensure their employees are
motivated so they can support the organization.

To conclude, we can say that motivation ultimately influences employees to behave in the way they behave in the workplace. Every organization must focus on their employee motivation to be able to have a competitive advantage. Motivation is one of the vital factors for the organizations, along with the globalization concern, environmental stability, etc. If motivational theories are applied to an organization, it will help companies have positive and open-minded employees who are positively motivated to impact the results of the organizations and gain competitive advantage. In the end, it ensures a productive high-performing organization.

Quiz

1. **Organizations use resources and labor to motivate employees to alter their behavior to benefit _____, _____, and _____.**

   a. the organization, the company, the corporation

   b. the worker, the customer, the employee

   c. the customer, the investor, the entrepreneur

   d. the organization, the employee, the customer

2. **Reinforcement is responding to behavior; motivation is the feeling in the individual.**

   a. True

   b. False

3. **Positive reinforcement is _____.**

   a. responding to a behavior with a reward.

   b. responding to a behavior by removing a privilege.

   c. responding to a behavior with a punishment.

   d. responding to a behavior by removing an undesirable circumstance.

4. Negative reinforcement is _____.

a. responding to a behavior with a reward

b. responding to a behavior by removing a privilege

c. responding to a behavior with a punishment

d. responding to a behavior by removing an undesirable circumstance

5. Positive punishment is _____.

a. responding to a behavior with a reward

b. responding to a behavior by removing a privilege

c. responding to a behavior with a punishment

d. responding to a behavior by removing an undesirable circumstance

6. Negative punishment is _____.

a. responding to a behavior with a reward

b. responding to a behavior by removing a privilege

c. responding to a behavior with a punishment

d. responding to a behavior by removing an undesirable circumstance

7. **Extinction of behavior is _____.**

   a. the decrease of a behavior that changed to gain a reward

   b. the decrease of a behavior that is undesirable

   c. the decrease of a behavior that is desirable

   d. the increase of a behavior that is undesirable

8. **Intrinsic motivation is _____.**

   a. motivation based on internal factors

   b. motivation based on external factors

   c. motivation based on friends

   d. motivation based on family

9. **Extrinsic motivation is _____.**

   a. motivation based on internal factors

   b. motivation based on external factors

   c. motivation based on a sense of accomplishment

   d. motivation based on emotions

10. Charging every employee an extra $50 on their health insurance plan until and unless they sign a form promising not to use tobacco products is an example of _____.

a. positive reinforcement

b. negative reinforcement

c. positive punishment

d. negative punishment

Answers	1 – d	2 – a	3 – a	4 – d	5 – c
	6 – b	7 – a	8 – a	9 – b	10 – b

Chapter Summary

Organizations need to use resources and labor to motivate employees and alter behavior to benefit the organization, the employee, or the customer--sometimes all three. There are many approaches to motivation and reinforcement. Some employees seem to do the right thing without being told. The right thing in the context of organizations is generally a mixture of what is best for the employee, the organization, and the customer. Finding a way to maximize the benefit to all parties involved is a constant struggle. Business goals change, customer needs evolve, and employee needs are not always causally linked to their behavior. Reinforcement theory is more nuanced than it seems on first glance. First, positive and negative reinforcement do not refer to desired and undesired consequences for behavior; they refer to actively inflicting a consequence on an employee or withholding or removing a consequence. This is further broken down by punishment, which also has a positive and negative side; positive punishment is a response to behavior and negative punishment is the withholding of an undesirable stimulus. An example of positive reinforcement is a bonus for exceeding a goal. An example of negative reinforcement is having to pay $50 extra on a health insurance plan, but as soon as the employee signs a promise not to use tobacco products, the $50 is removed from the cost of the health insurance plan. They are both reinforcement because they are desirable to the employee. Punishment is experiencing undesirable consequences. An example of a positive punishment is fine for breaking an organizational rule. An example of negative punishment is requiring employees to work mandatory overtime unless a goal is reached; if employees dislike mandatory overtime, then they will work harder to reach the goal so they can end the unpleasant work conditions. Extinction of behavior is usually an unintended consequence of rewards systems. If each sales employee sells 100 units per day, then the company offers a 10% bonus for employees to sell 115 units per day, reinforcement theory would expect this positive reinforcement to result in an overall increase in sales. However, if after three months, the management team decides it is too expensive to keep this incentive in place they might cancel the 10% bonus program. Some managers might assume sales figures that were at a new, higher plateau would maintain, but reinforcement theory suggests that sales will fall to the original 100 units per day or possibly further. Motivation theory overlaps with reinforcement theory somewhat, but there are key differences. Reinforcement is about someone in control issuing consequences for behavior. Motivation is about the internal impulses of the individual. The two main theories of motivation are extrinsic and intrinsic motivation. Extrinsic is external motivation such as rewards that come from others. Intrinsic is internal motivation, which comes from within and can be for a variety of reasons. Great leaders can help employees develop goals, which can drive behavior in a more intrinsic way. Highly effective organizations strike a useful balance between positive and negative reinforcement and punishment; they also work to develop intrinsic and extrinsic motivation when possible. Creating an environment conducive to great leadership and motivation helps to maximum effectiveness.

This page is intentionally left blank

Chapter 4

Perceptions, Decision-Making, and Problem Solving

Some coworkers and managers repeat the old cliché, "perception is reality." There is some truth to this idea. Although the way we perceive things is not actually the same as reality, nor does it directly influence reality, it does influence how we behave. This means that the way people perceive us is the way they will treat us and the way we perceive others strongly influences how we treat them. People dressed in clean, neat, formal clothing tend to be perceived as more respectable than people who wear dirty, torn, or casual clothing. People who frequently arrive late to work and meetings tend to be perceived as irresponsible and uncommitted while people who arrive early seem organized and responsible. These perceptions do not reflect the reality of a person's skill or ability to contribute to the organization, but will usually affect decisions made about them including their career opportunities.

Decisions constantly demand attention throughout the day. We do not have time to carefully consider every decision we make, especially unimportant ones that do not greatly impact our lives. Other decisions are so important that we must carefully consider them for hours or days to make sure we make the best choice. Challenges present themselves throughout the day beginning with going to work and continuing through getting back home at the end of the day. How efficiently and effectively we solve problems will determine the quality of our life and the amount of time we have to do things we enjoy. Organizations face challenges and employees good at problem solving are more likely to earn respect and be given more responsibilities. Perceptions, decision-making, and problem solving are important parts of organizational life.

What will be covered in this chapter

- Perception and behavior

- Problem solving steps including (define the problem and its significance, analyze the "why" of the problem, gather relevant data and impact of the problem across business units, how leadership team can work together to solve the problem, implement the solution, evaluate and monitor the solution)

- Decision making steps including (define the issue, collect relevant data, make the decision, monitor and evaluate)

Psychology and perceptions help manage the employees in an organization. Psychological principles are applied to employee behaviors and emotions that ultimately make or break organizational cultures. When managers deal with employees fairly, it makes the job satisfying and interesting for the employees; they are better motivated resulting in higher productivity at work. Attitude is the complex mixture of underlying feelings, emotions, beliefs and values that we call personality. Attitudes help us define how we view, and behave in, any given situation. Basically, our beliefs and feelings determine our actions. Perceptions are closely connected to attitudes and are a process of how we see things and form our opinions about them.

4.1 Perceptions and Behavior

Perceptions are reality to some people in the workplace. People do not act according to reality; they act according to their perception of reality. If a supervisor perceives an employee as capable, that employee will receive additional responsibilities, and through time, become more capable. Some supervisors award raises and promotions based on their perception of employees rather than reality. If employees perceive an office as hostile, their defensive behavior may cause coworkers to act more guarded and the perception becomes a self-fulfilling prophecy. Another way perception becomes reality is that most people do not analyze their perceptions. Most of the time, all perceptions are grouped together in the mind; the uneasy feeling around a certain coworker is mixed with the perception of reality that walls keep out weather and it is safe to sit in chairs. The uneasy feeling could be a legitimate warning of a dangerous person, but it is more likely an error in perception. An employee could be intimidated by someone's job title or accomplishments or it could be an underlying negative stereotype.

Employee perceptions have a direct link to their behaviors in the workplace. Employees with a positive perception of the work environment can influence behavior and motivation. However, this works both ways; employees with a negative perception of the work culture will be demotivated and resistant to change. Negative perceptions of the employees can create a hostile work environment with bullying, harassment, and conflict. In the globalized work dynamics, understanding the perceptions and how the workplace is influenced by these negative or positive perceptions helps employees to develop and influence their behaviors. Human resource professionals can benefit from strengthening conflict-resolution training in the workplace to mitigate some of the risks of negative perceptions.

Individual differences are an important element of organizational behavior. They not only shape the overall organizational culture but they help with the success of the organization. Positive individual attributes and perceptions help embrace change in the organization. Employees bring several differences to work including their varied personalities, values, and attitudes about the organization. When a new hire joins the organization, their characteristics affect how they behave and perform in a workplace along with their knowledge, skills, and abilities.

Perceptions of the workplace can be changed and embraced by different personality traits. Personality traits are described by different personality characteristics like curiosity, intellect,

ambition, sensitivity, attentiveness, optimism, humor, etc.
Personality is one of the important factors in predicting the work
behavior of the employee. Companies try to assess the candidate's
personality as a potential good match for the organizational
culture. Many organizations also use personality testing as a
prerequisite of employment. Companies believe that using these
testing improves their recruitment selection and reduces turnover.

The perception process typically illustrates the basic
framework or elements where each person or individual chooses
and responds differently. Understanding the different behaviors
and personalities helps managers understand why people behave
differently at work. With the globalization context, companies
are trying to balance and improve the financial performance
and organizations with wise leadership who will focus more
on performance than individual differences. With these kinds
of global impacts in mind, companies and their workforces
must be willing to collaborate with each other in order to be
productive. There is a close link between attitudes, decision
making, and problem solving at the workplace. Employees with
positive attitudes at work often contribute to problem solving in
organizations. They are proactive high performers who support
the organization's key decisions and speak up if they have a
different opinion.

4.2 Problem Solving

Solving problems is a valuable skill in the workplace. When
a problem appears it is an opportunity to quickly solve it and
continue with work or to investigate further and see if there

is potential to spend more time and energy to prevent similar problems in the future. Much of what business leaders do is to make the decisions whether to solve it or change the underlying factors that caused the problem. It is important to define the problem prior to jumping to the conclusion. If the problem is overwhelming, break it into small manageable steps and try creating quick wins. The struggle is that people often react to the problem by seeing what it is instead of asking why there is a problem in the first place. Another key aspect of problem solving is prioritizing problems into urgent and important ones. A business leader's role can greatly influence how they perceive the role of others in problem solving. Problem solving is the core of leadership. Leaders are responsible for minimizing the problems in an organization and they must have insight to foresee situations before they become the problem and courage to address them. Leaders play an extremely critical role in creative problem solving. For any organization to be successful and prosper, constant improvement in efficient processes and creative products are needed. Leaders must have the ability to stimulate change and inspire their teams to be creative with decision making and their problem-solving approach to fuel their organization's growth and success.

There are some proven problem-solving strategies of business leaders to create high-performance customer-centric organizations.

In times of crisis, it is the responsibility of the business leaders to be transparent and communicate clearly with their teams. Great leaders are also great problem solvers. They work on breaking down the silos that frequently arise from organizational boundaries. Additionally, business leaders work on creating an open-minded culture that helps people to serve customers and impact the growth of the organization. They usually have a plan of action when it comes to business decisions. We will see in the next section how problem-solving leadership impacts powerful decision-making ability for leadership in a high-performing organization.

Figure 4.1 **Problem solving method**

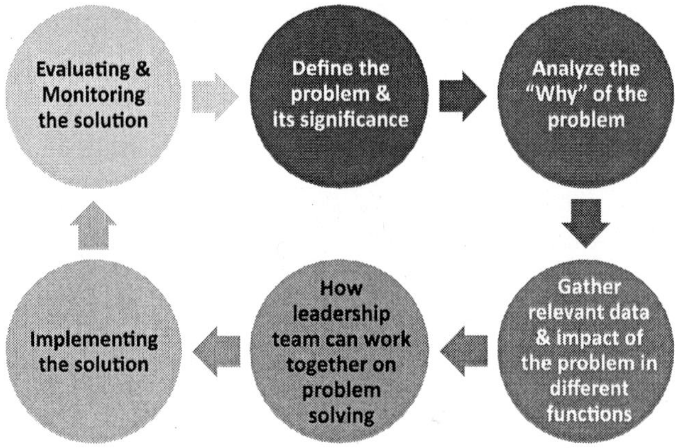

4.3 Decision Making

Decision making in a global high-performing organization happens at all levels. Decision making is about deciding what action to take in any given situation. In more hierarchical organizations, decisions are made at the top but a flatter and high-performing global company believes in the autonomy of employees to make decisions for faster responses. However, there is a process in place which employees usually have to follow.

For example, companies may have a four-eye principle for any decisions which means at least two people must be part of any given decision and a cosigner is needed for every contract or agreement. One employee may not be allowed to make decisions based on his or her preference. Any business leader who aspires to excellence will have a vested interest in making the best business decisions. The leader will empower their team to ensure best and optimal decisions that benefit the company. Every member of the organization must be engaged in achieving business goals.

4.4 Decision Making Framework

Decision making framework has some key factors to consider like defining goals, collecting relevant data prior to making a decision, evaluating suitable options, making a decision, implementing the decision, and evaluating the results.

Defining the objective or the goal in any given situation is an important element and first step of decision making. Individuals or teams must understand what they are trying to achieve and why.

Figure 4.2 | **Decision Making Framework that correlates with Problem Solving**

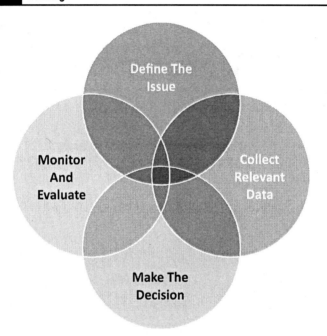

Collecting all relevant information related to the objective in this framework is an important step. Collecting the data and evaluating the data to reach a goal is important for any business.

The third step would be to ultimately decide with help of all the data gathered. This will enable the business leader to make a sound, data-driven decision.

Implementing the decision and evaluating the results is the last but most important step. This helps with lessons learned and improves the quality of decisions made in the future.

Quiz

1. How do perceptions differ from reality?

  a. There is no difference

  b. Perceptions are more important than reality

  c. Reality is how things actually are; Perceptions are how people interpret reality

  d. Perceptions are unimportant

2. What might contribute to someone's perception of a situation.

  a. Being in a similar situation in the past

  b. Preconceived ideas and stereotypes

  c. Strong, deeply-held beliefs

  d. All of the above

3. What are the 4 steps of problem solving in this chapter?

  a. Evaluate results, monitor results, gather data, make a decision

  b. Gather data, identify a problem, monitor results, make a decision

  c. Make a decision, gather data, identify a problem, evaluate results

  d. Define the issue, collect relevant data, make the decision, monitor and evaluate results

4. What are personality traits that might affect one's perception?

a. Curiosity and intellect

b. Sensitivity and ambition

c. Attentiveness and optimism

d. All of the above

5. Companies often try to assess a candidate's _____ through mandatory tests as a potential good match for the organizational culture.

a. personality

b. leadership

c. height

d. writing

6. Employees with a positive attitude often _____ problem solving in organizations.

a. neglect

b. contribute to

c. combat

d. detract from

7. **If a problem is overwhelming, _____.**

   a. give up immediately

   b. try and then give up

   c. tell someone else to do it

   d. break it into manageable steps

8. **In times of crisis, it is the responsibility of the business leaders to _____ with their teams.**

   a. communicate clearly

   b. part

   c. undermine

   d. dine

9. **Why is defining the objective or goal in a situation so important?**

   a. It is good to know things

   b. Individuals or teams must understand what they are trying to achieve and why

   c. Definitions impact results

   d. It creates a quick win

10. Part of competing in a global market is the ability to see and react to environmental factors _____ the competition.

   a. as well as

   b. much slower and deliberate

   c. with more enthusiasm

   d. more quickly and efficiently than

Answers	1 – c	2 – d	3 – d	4 – d	5 – a
	6 – b	7 – d	8 – a	9 – b	10 – d

Chapter Summary

Perceptions are opinions formed through observation of one's surroundings. Perceptions influence how people treat others and how others treat them in return. There are several interactions that take place at work and these perceptions are influenced by a variety of different factors like culture, leadership behaviors, diversity within the organization, etc. The behaviors exhibited by employees are influenced by how they are treated or what they see in the workplace. Employees usually behave in similar ways to their supervisors and coworkers. Learning about employee perceptions and interactions in a work environment helps business leaders and human resource professionals understand motivation levels, employee engagement, and cultural impact. Problem solving is a big part of leadership. Part of competing in a global market is the ability to see and react to environmental factors more quickly and efficiently than the competition. Understanding problems is vital to properly solving them. The deeper the understanding of the problem, the stronger the foundation of the solution. Categorizing problems is important. Identifying the urgent and important ones allows leaders to solve them first and keep the organization performing at maximum efficiency. Less urgent problems are also important. It is necessary to address them for the long-term success of the organization. Successful organizations need to consistently improve their processes. Excellent problem solvers can improve their organizations growth and success. After identifying the cause of a problem, a solution must be implemented to solve the problem. There are usually multiple methods to solve a problem and a decision must be made to determine which way to proceed. Decision making is a skill that can be learned and improved through study and practice. With experience, leaders can make a decision quickly and it usually turns out to be the best way to proceed. It is important to gather results and analyze data of past decisions. This helps with the quality of future decisions.

This page is intentionally left blank

Chapter 5

Theories in Talent Development

Organizations with talented, highly-skilled, well-trained employees are more likely to succeed than organizations that do not take a proactive approach to cultivating capable employees. This chapter will cover talent development theories including business needs, justification of training, creation and implementation of talent development programs, and evaluating training effectiveness. Types of training methods and specific models will be covered including classroom, eLearning, on-the-job training, ADDIE, the Kirkpatrick Model as well as globalization and its impact on talent development.

What will be covered in this chapter

- The importance and justification of talent development and training

- ADDIE: Analysis, Design, Development,
  Implementation, Evaluation
- The Kirkpatrick Model of training evaluation
- The globalization of training

5.1 Talent Development and Training

Talent development is the process of improving the employees within an organization, usually with the objective to improve the organization. Large corporations often have dedicated talent development executives, departments, managers, teams, and individual contributors, each with a unique skill set. This makes up a learning and development (L&D) or training department. Sometimes this is structured under the corporate human resources department and is responsible for all talent development in the organization. Sometimes this is structured under operations as a training and development department reporting to, and specializing in issues directly related to, that operational division. This can look very different in large organizations, but some common trends are to have the following positions filled with highly specialized professionals: training manager, instructional designer, technical writer, and trainer. They all play an integral part in creating effective training and development programs with classrooms, training materials, communications, etc. In large organizations and especially in areas with high turnover, classes of five to twenty-five participants could occur every few weeks all year long. Trainers are in classes all day every day for weeks at a time and rarely get a week away from training to perform other duties within the organization. When trainers report to work without a class to teach, they usually spend time practicing what they teach, such as participating in manufacturing duties or taking calls in a call center, or they review course materials looking for outdated or inaccurate information. Technical writers and instructional designer/developers (IDD) work all day to create training content such as participant guides (PG), facilitator guides (FG), web-based training (WBT) or computer-based training (CBT), sequence of event (SOE) documents, tip sheets, signs, and anything else that will help the organization, especially the training department.

Small organizations look very different from this. It would not make financial sense to have four different positions for talent development if it doubled or tripled the size of the entire organization. In such cases there is often one person with a job title similar to "training coordinator" who essentially does the work of all four positions. This person acts as a training manager by meeting with people responsible for different duties or departments to determine training and development needs. Training coordinators act as a technical writer by documenting processes and sequences of events (SOE), and as an instructional designer/developer (IDD) by putting the instructions, descriptions, and pictures together into a training document or program that can be taught. This person often acts as the trainer by onboarding new hires and giving them all the information about organizational policies and procedures, benefits, and job-specific guidance and education. This kind of training is often one-on-one and fairly infrequent.

Not all organizations without a dedicated talent development or training department are small. Some organizations did not see the value in a training department. Their onboarding process for new hires looks very different. If a new hire is lucky, the person leaving a position will work for a week or two to train the new hire in an on-the-job-training (OJT) manner. If the new hire is unlucky, there will be a difficult learning curve with many bumps along the way and a lot of trial and error until the position is figured out. This method is less disruptive in a position where mistakes are acceptable. However, for highly technical or public-facing jobs more focus, time, and consideration are given to new employees so the company does not have to worry about their reputation being marred by egregious errors or sued by victims of faulty products. Another possibility is a job position where multiple people perform the same duties. In this case, OJT is conducted by an experienced employee who is a subject matter expert (SME). Sometimes the SME is good at relaying the information. Sometimes the SME can only demonstrate the skill and hope the new hire learns by watching.

5.1.1 Justifying Talent Development and Training

In today's quickly evolving business landscape, training new and existing employees is a big challenge; but what makes it more challenging is trying to convince leadership to invest in training and development (Nathan, 2018). This is an ongoing issue in many organizations. While some organizations see the value in learning and development programs, others do not. Leaders do not see the value that a training department would add to the organization; they only see the cost. Tony Bingham, CEO of ATD, asserts that talent development in organizations contributes to lasting market leadership because they drive organizational agility, innovation, and growth (LinkedIn, 2018). In addition to the benefits to all participating employees, leaders can benefit from development.

5.1.2 Leadership Development

Although it's true that some natural leadership tendencies are innate, nobody is a born leader. "Everyone, however, can develop leadership skills. And everyone can benefit from focused and deliberate development" (Leadership, 2020). Leaders do not learn everything they need in a single event so ongoing development is necessary. It takes time to shed unproductive habits and build better ones. It is impossible to prepare a leader for every situation that may arise. A better way to build strong leaders is to develop their leadership skills over time with repetition. Sadly, leaders often do not see the value in development for themselves or their teams.

5.1.3 Training Creation and Implementation

Training creation and implementation includes multiple steps. First someone identifies a training, then someone gathers information and designs a training program to meet the needs, then someone develops the training program. This is the basic process for the creation of training. Implementation is when the training program is rolled out to employees or learners and this can include pre-tests, classroom or online training classes or modules, and examinations. Some people consider training complete at this point, but there is another important step: evaluation of training. The purpose of the evaluation is to gauge training effectiveness, identify opportunities for improvement, reporting to leadership and other stakeholders, and improvement for the next iteration of the training program. This is one of the most widely used and respected processes for training and development programs in the business world. ADDIE (Analysis, Design, Development, Implementation, and Evaluation) is the most familiar model for this process. The Kirkpatrick Model is the most respected model for the evaluation phase of ADDIE.

5.2 ADDIE - Analysis

ADDIE (Analysis, Design, Development, Implementation, and Evaluation) has been used since the 1970s in organizations including the military, businesses, and schools. During the analysis phase, leaders will consider factors including the reason for training, the characteristics of the learner, and the ideal delivery method. The reason for training is usually a training need. This can be a gap between expectation and performance, a new process, a new product, or a new tool. One of the most important pieces of information in this step is the difference between what the learner already knows and what the learner is expected to know after the training. Sometimes this is called the delta, named after the fourth letter of the greek alphabet Δ used as a mathematical term for change. For example, if an employee needs to know ten things to be successful, and already knows eight, then the delta is two. This means the employee needs to learn two things to be successful. However, if an employee only knows four of the ten requirements for success, then the delta is six and the employee must learn six things to be successful. Knowing the delta or training gap is important for efficiency. It would be inefficient to cover all ten things in the training if the learner knows nine of the ten things and only one thing is missing.

For example, if the only gap between current performance and expectation is knowing that the company issued a new rule that it will no longer accept returns on a specific product, then the employee could obtain that information in an email and still be successful.

If the training gap is that the company has a new model or version of its product that just became available then a spec sheet might be the most useful tool. It could include illustrations of the product from different angles with specifications and features listed on the same page. This requires almost no training time for employees to be successful. On the other hand, if a call center agent in a billing department will be required to use a new software to search for customer information, take payments, and look up past, curent, and future billing details, then an email or spec sheet will not be sufficient for the learner to be successful. In this case, there needs to be a training program developed and delivered that covers everything from logging in to the new software to where all of the responsibilities and information can be found. In this case the delta or training gap is only the specific software features and locations of tools to perform necessary duties. The learner does not need to learn the company's policy on billing, only where to find the customer's bill in the new system.

5.3 ADDIE - Design

Design can begin after a thorough analysis. The design phase considers the learning method or location (e.g. online or classroom), strategies for introducing learning objectives identified during analysis, and a plan for how it will be measured for success. Measuring successfulness of training programs is the final step in the process: evaluation. Good design accounts for the need for evaluation and builds that into the framework for the program. For example, one method for evaluating learning is to compare scores of a pre-test and final exam. The percentage of improvement can be considered as the amount of learning that took place. However if a pre-test was not designed and developed, then when the last step is considered, it is too late to add the pre-test for the first group of learners. Development, implementation, and evaluation go much smoother when the design phase is thorough.

Just like some training programs could have simply been an email, it is important to design the level of intensity and time required for mastery of the new information or skill. Sometimes a three-minute microlearning online course will suffice and operations managers would prefer this, if possible, because it can be accomplished by employees arriving five minutes early or staying five minutes late. The added payroll expense is small. On the other hand, training new hires in a complex skill set, requires more substantial methods. This could be as simple as a one-day training and orientation to go over company policies, safety procedures, and basic job skills; or it could be as involved as a classroom experience with a dedicated trainer and several participants going through multiple lectures, eLearning modules, written exercises, tests, and observation of successful employees, stretched out over several weeks. The more intricate training programs usually have a very detailed schedule that outlines how many minutes or hours each learning objective should take. This helps a trainer stay on task, helps prevent information overload due to a fast pace, or limits learner boredom from the slow pacing of the program. This is also the step where an instructional designer/developer (IDD) would interview or observe a subject matter expert doing the task or demonstrating the skill.

The design phase also involves a rough idea of how individual parts of the training might look. This gives stakeholders such as operations managers and executive leadership a chance to give feedback or voice concerns over part of the program before it is fully developed. Once it is fully developed a lot of time has been wasted if the module is not used and some leaders will include it in the overall curriculum because it is already created and it is not very bad. Some of the early meetings or communications would include storyboards with basic illustrations and outlines of the training objectives and the order they will be presented. Feedback at this stage is crucial because it saves time in the long run.

5.4 ADDIE - Development

Development of a training program is the step most people imagine when thinking of training creation. This is when an instructional designer/developer (IDD) writes a user manual, creates a tip sheet, organizes a sequence of events (SOE) document, takes screenshots of important steps, creates tests or exams online or on paper, or creates an interactive training simulation for an eLearning module. Once the document or module or tip sheet or SOE has been created, it is shown to beta testers who will give feedback to improve the training before it is launched. Beta testers will usually attempt to follow along in the training material while performing the actions in the real world to test if steps are missing or inadequately explained. The more iterations of testing and feedback from people that help with refining the training, the more polished the final product will be. In the development phase an IDD will often include a short refresher of previously learned material and a post-learning quiz to test understanding of the course. Once it is fully developed a course is ready to be implemented.

5.5 ADDIE - Implementation and Evaluation

Implementation is the phase when the final preparations are performed and the training is launched. This is the phase when websites are tested, train-the-trainer (T3) sessions are conducted, classroom space is secured (if needed), and time away from regular duties for learners is scheduled including finding coverage. When the training begins, there is usually more oversight and attention due to the excitement of the desired success. After a few iterations of the process, then leaders follow up on the training results mainly through periodic reports.

The final step is evaluation. Evaluation is the phase where stakeholders gauge how effective the program was, whether to continue it, how to change it if it continues, and other decisions based on organizational needs. This phase of ADDIE is usually left out of training initiatives if the organization is new to formal talent development or unaware of the benefits of this last step. Although every phase of ADDIE has its own evaluation, it is called formative evaluation. The final evaluation, or the summary of the training program as a whole, is called summative evaluation. It is so important it will be given its own section under the well-known Kirkpatrick Model.

5.6 Kirkpatrick Model

The Kirkpatrick Model was developed in the 1950s by Dr. Donald Kirkpatrick. It has been used ever since to demonstrate training effectiveness and value to organizations.

It has four levels:

- **Reaction** - Did participants like it and find it useful?

- **Learning** - Did participants learn the knowledge or gain the skills?

- **Behavior** - Did participants apply the new knowledge or skills to their jobs after training?

- **Results** - Did the planned organizational objectives succeed?

The levels increase in complexity and time required to complete. This correlates to the frequency of their use. Sometimes as an afterthought, participants will be asked how they thought the training went, whether they found it useful, and other questions about their reaction to the training. Sometimes the trainer will be asked how it went and whether there were any difficulties or issues leaders need to know. For some organizations and email or survey is the only feedback or evaluation they get for the training.

Level 1 Reaction

It is important to understand the training program on this level. Although enjoyment of a course does not guarantee learning, if participants dislike it they are less likely to want to learn and put forth effort and less likely to want to participate in the next training session. Questions for participants include their reaction to the trainer, the technology, the supplemental material, and whether the training was useful to their job.

Level 2 Learning

This is usually an examination of some kind whether a test or observing new skills or desired behavior as it is demonstrated by learners. The best way to gauge the level of learning success is through a pretest and a post-test. The difference between the scores is the amount of learning that can reasonably be attributed to the training.

Level 3 Evaluation

This step is more about behavior than knowledge. It is best to wait three to six months to see whether, and how, the employees behave differently. It takes time to master a new skill or properly incorporate new information into one's routine. Waiting a few months to see if participants are using what they learned is the best way to measure this level of learning. It can be done through observation or testing and evaluators must exercise great care to ensure they are properly measuring the impact of the training and not inadvertently including another variable that contributed to new behavior.

Level 4 Results

This is usually the reason the training was proposed in the first place. This is usually a measurement of the planned learning objectives. Examples include increased sales, reduced call handling time, fewer accidents, and higher quality of products manufactured. To properly attribute a result to the training and not environmental or market factors, it is important to have a control group of employees who did not participate in the training program. Then measurable Key Performance Indicators (KPI) can be compared between the group of employees who received the training and those who did not. If these KPIs are easily attached to organizational revenue, profit, or savings, then it is possible to calculate a Return on Investment (ROI) for the training program.

Consider this example of ROI based on training effectiveness. An organization has used the same work safety training module for ten years and the number of accidents has remained steady over that decade. Then a new training module is introduced that replaces the old one. Within a few months the number of accidents has decreased by thirty percent. The new training module is used for another six months. Six months later, the number of accidents is still thirty percent lower than in previous years. This is an example of level four: results. The organization can calculate the cost of workers' compensation claims, medical bills, lost time, etc., and then calculate the cost to the organization. This calculation can be performed for the cost to the company when it used the previous training module and compare it to the cost to the company after it began using the new training module. The difference could be attributed to the effectiveness of the training. If the company paid $20,000 for the new training but saved $350,000 in the first year after the training, then the return on investment (ROI) is clear. The difficulty is when the training is for soft skills or change management and influencing employee perceptions of a new policy. Sometimes it is more difficult to quantify the value of training, which is why some companies do not see any value in training at all and do not invest in a training department or hiring training consultants.

5.7 Globalization of Training

Global organizations can benefit from globalizing their training. This includes altering their current curriculum or even creating a new one. New training should be aware of cultural differences, different languages or dialects of the primary language, and other regional or local considerations. It is important to include a native speaker of the language the training will be translated into so the training does not make mistakes like using offensive words that are considered normal in the company where the company is headquartered. Preferred learning styles is important to consider such as certain parts of the globe are more receptive to Instructor-Led Training (ILT) which usually takes place in a classroom, while other parts of the world are less receptive to this method and prefer alternatives such as eLearning modules or On-the-Job Training (OJT). The benefits of globalizing training include increased participation and understanding and increased perception of respect and consideration for the new region and its employees.

Quiz

1. **What is ADDIE?**

   a. A method for creating advertisement designs and drafts

   b. A method for designing drafts of international exploration

   c. A method for analysis, design, development, implementation, and evaluation of a training program

   d. A method for analyzing, designing, and drafting intellectual enterprises

2. **What does the Kirkpatrick Method measure?**

   a. Training effectiveness

   b. Leadership development

   c. Computer skills

   d. Intelligence

3. **What does OJT mean?**

   a. Order Job Transfer

   b. Over Job Training

   c. On the Job Training

   d. Old Job Transfer

4. Where would a learner find CBT or WBT training?

a. In a textbook or pamphlet

b. On a poster or sign

c. On a computer, phone, or tablet

d. In a classroom or lecture hall

5. What does ILT mean?

a. Interlaced Training

b. Inversion Light Testing

c. Infinite Lasting Training

d. Instructor Led Training

6. What are the 4 steps of the Kirkpatrick Model?

a. Training, testing, studying, practicing

b. Reaction, learning , behavior, results

c. Learning, reactions, results, behavior

d. Behavior, results, learning, action

7. What does KPI stand for?

a. Kirkpatrick Price Index

b. Key Performance Indicator

c. Knowledgeable Paper Interest

d. Keystrokes Per Inch

8. **What does T3 stand for?**

   a. Train-The-Trainer

   b. Take-The-Test

   c. Test-The-Timing

   d. Thoroughly-Tested-Trainer

9. **What does SOE stand for?**

   a. Serious or Enjoyable

   b. Sequence of Events

   c. Stable over Everything

   d. Situations of Environmentalism

10. **What does IDD stand for?**

   a. Inter-Demonstration Design

   b. Intra-Development Density

   c. Investigation Dealer Device

   d. Instructional Designer/Developer

Answers	1 – c	2 – a	3 – c	4 – c	5 – d
	6 – b	7 – b	8 – a	9 – b	10 – d

Chapter Summary

Learning and development is a valuable addition to any organization. Whether it is a new employee, a new department, a consultant, or a new module purchased from a third-party vendor it is good to develop people in an organization; and the better the people are, the better the organization can be. Training development is often structured according to ADDIE using the Kirkpatrick Model for the evaluation phase. The more clear the learning objectives are during the analysis phase, the easier the entire process will be and the better the changes are of giving the operational leaders a definitive ROI figure. Taking care to involve more stakeholders in the design and development phases will allow implementation to move forward with as few trouble as possible. Whether or not a specific dollar figure of increased earnings or savings can be calculated, employees usually feel more valued, respected, and nurtured if they are included in regular high-quality training programs.

Chapter **6**

Group Behavior, Teamwork and High-Performance Teams

This chapter covers group behavior, teamwork, and examples of how teams help organizations succeed. Individuals working together make up a group; and groups working together make up an organization. One of the most well-known group behavior models was created by Bruce Tuckman in 1965. It consists of four stages: Forming, Storming, Norming, and Performing. In 1977 Tuckman and Mary Ann Jensen added a fifth stage: Adjourning.

What will be covered in this chapter

- Tuckman's stages of team development: forming, storming, norming, performing, adjourning

- Cultural differences

- Qualities of high-performing teams
- Talent acquisition
- Rewards and motivation
- Leadership and communication
- Empowering teams

6.1 Stage 1: Forming

In this stage the individuals are introduced and treat each other as strangers. Meetings are polite and the individuals attempt to get to know each other and get along. This stage is usually short.

6.2 Stage 2: Storming

In this stage the individuals begin to introduce conflicting opinions and some fight for control or influence. This stage offers the opportunity to get to know team members better and even work toward building trust. As people open up about ideas, conflicts occur. Team members must resolve these conflicts and learn to respect each other before they can move on to the next stage. Some teams never progress past this stage.

6.3 Stage 3: Norming

In this stage the individuals tolerate personality differences and idiosyncrasies. Cooperation becomes routine and the individuals become a close-knit group. Sometimes controversial opinions pull the group back into stage 2: storming. Individuals know this so some will not share potentially controversial opinions. This keeps the group working congenially, but it may stifle creativity and perhaps hurt performance in the long run.

6.4 Stage 4: Performing

In this stage individuals begin to focus more on the needs of the group and accomplishing goals than their own individual desires. They are more willing to accept another person's ideas as superior to their own and the group can begin to succeed at surprising levels. Groups in this stage can make most of their own decisions and require little oversight from a manager.

Figure 6.1   **Four Stages of Group Formation**

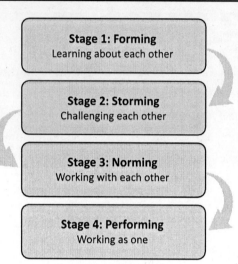

6.5 Stage 5: Adjourning

Group dynamics change. Members come and go. Managers get reassigned to new groups. Groups succeed in their objective that brought the group together in the first place. There are many reasons the group breaks up, but eventually they all do. This stage is sometimes called "mourning."

There are many stages of group development, but high-performing groups, or teams, are the backbone of any organization.

A team is much more effective than an individual or even a group of individuals working near each other. Collaborating, sharing, and working together achieves much better results because teams are more effective than individuals. It takes time to learn to trust each other and work together effectively, but the time it takes to become an effective team is saved through increased efficiency later. Human resource management practices can help teams achieve high-performance through effective talent management, learning and development programs, and rewards and incentives initiatives. High-performing teams put the goals of the organization above personal success. Talented teams are skilled at decision making and problem solving. Motivating a team and rewarding success are integral parts of organizational success. High-performing leaders set an example for their teams. They also guide their teams with a clear vision. Empowering employees by trusting them to make the right decisions allows them to overcome obstacles quickly without the need to ask a manager for advice or permission. This efficiency is good for the organization.

Teamwork can refer to a wide range of possibilities of working conditions, interactions with coworkers, collaboration with cross-functional teams, or virtual teams. Effective team management allows organizations to sustain today's and demanding business environment and globalization challenges. The high-performing teams are about team members and leaders who can manage teams into high stress with high-performance outcomes. Human Resource Management practices are creating strategies and effective reward systems to empower teams by involving them in key business decisions and plan their performance around their projects.

Effective teamwork affects organizational performance. Leadership and executive teams have credited teams for helping organizations reach profitability. Many organizations closely monitor the interrelation between team performance and output generated. Conflicts, complaints, grievances, or hostility are another key indicator of low morale. If a team doesn't have clarity about their role within a team or how they will interact with others, or if roles of other team members are unclear, this will create a lack of interest and lack of commitment to the team ultimately resulting in insufficient initiative, innovation, imagination, or risk taking.

Teams are groups of individuals who are interdependent to perform their tasks for effective team performance, team leadership and team participation. Development of teams and team building skills are extremely important due to the tremendous exposure of team working in the last decade. Most global organizations of Fortune 1000 companies are recruiting team players: the company's focus on building high-performing teams for efficiency in changing environments. Organizations use a variety of performance predictors such as team member roles, problem solving strategies, communication patterns, leadership actions, decision making quality, and productivity patterns.

Figure 6.2   Characteristics of High-Performance Teams

CHARACTERISTICS OF HIGH PERFORMANCE TEAM

- Innovative
- Foster Creativity
- Diverse and Inclusive
- Goal Oriented

- Self Directed
- Conflict Management
- High Morale
- Mutual Trust

- Effective Communication
- Cross - Functional Collaboration
- Embrace Change
- Visionary Leadership

6.6 Team Development

Team dynamics cause the team relationships to change and effective behaviors of leaders have a most impact on team dynamics. A High-Performing Team is imperative for continued business success and companies invest time and resources to ensure they have stable, high-performing teams. Creating a high-performing team is a demanding task for many organizations and to keep the team motivated in this ever-changing environment. Many organizations who have successfully embedded high-performance culture within their organizations, are involved in design thinking approach and implemented strategies that shape the high-performing teams. Companies that embrace high-performing culture within their organizations significantly outperform their competition.

There are many moving parts in creating high-performing teams. The dynamic nature of today's complex challenges with resource limitations, market competitiveness and continuous technology enhancements are all affecting the way teams operate. The goal of any organization is to maintain sustainability and meet business needs while dealing with changing globalization impacts. However, the human factor remains to be the key driving force in organizations and teamwork has become the most important element. Cross functional teams are important for ongoing business and success of the organizations. Companies recognize the importance of team culture and invest a significant amount of resources on improving team performance. Companies constantly explore new ways to engage, motivate employees and improve team performance to accomplish higher levels of outcomes.

Organizations cannot succeed with one person. Teams are the foundation of workplace success in today's volatile and changing markets. However not many people are comfortable working in teams; members of the team must build relationships, team culture, and common ground. Communication is the common ground and collaboration is the key to produce high-quality and result oriented outcomes.

6.7 Cultural Differences

Global organizations are responsible for managing people from different cultures. Understanding and influencing teamwork in the context of building effective and efficient teams is the critical aspect of a high-performing organization. A high-performing work team is a group of individuals focused on accomplishing a goal or task: sharing expertise and skill to collaborate, innovate and deliver result-oriented outcomes. Organizations who strive for performance excellence, shared leadership goals, collaboration, openness, clear expectations, accountability, and trust within their team culture are able to outperform their competitors.

Human Resource Management (HRM) practices can help teams achieve high-performance by effective talent management, learning and development, conflict resolution strategies, diversity and inclusion cultures, and reward programs. High-Performance work teams are the new normal of globalized cultural environments. Executive leadership team strives for excellence when creating new products or services. New matrix teams are created for efficient product or service deliveries to customers.

Marketing and sales teams work together to generate a lead to sale conversions.

One of the significant differences of the high-performing teams from other teams is the individuals have a deep sense of purpose and commitment to the company's mission. They hold each other accountable and there is a clear sense of responsibility among team members. Teams are diversified and their expertise complements each other; and there is not only interdependence but also trust between the team members. Companies who create high-performance teams are at an advantage because each team member brings new ideas and skills to the table. They work on creating and executing strategy, accomplishing goals with little or no leadership direction because they are empowered to make their decisions and held accountable for the outcomes. Similarly, compensation structure is tied to the performance with an emphasis on collaborative team performance.

6.8 Qualities of High-Performing Teams

For decades, there are many measurable tools developed to measure team performance effectiveness, however, there seems to be a common base in understanding quality of effective teams. High-performance teams have many characteristics that help them succeed. They have goals and a purpose. This is usually given by leaders, but high-performing teams are capable of reassessing needs as they go and adjusting as required. They have good communication and camaraderie. Through mutual trust they feel closer and speak more freely with less fear of misunderstanding; they know that even if a misunderstanding occurs it will be quickly cleared up without offense or grudges. They have accountability and responsibility. Once a high-performing team is set on a path they will get the job done no matter what happens. One reason high-performing teams succeed regardless of obstacles is because team members have complementary skills, talents and abilities. Where one team member is weak another is strong. No matter what task is required someone on the team is capable. Whenever something threatens to thwart the mission someone rises to the challenge and keeps the team on track. Team members can accomplish their goals and have a sense of purpose around each task and they understand how these tasks relate to the entire organization's vision and values. It is important for leadership to clarify the purpose for their teams, so they understand how they fit into the organization's success.

6.9 Talent Acquisition

Leadership teams begin with talent acquisition and recruiting the best talent while also supporting low performers to excel and challenging them to perform their best. While high performers may come across as intimidating, it is important to realize for organizations that a high-performing team also raises the caliber of the entire organization. After the talent selection, it is critical to ensure that they also possess empathy and inclusivity. This will help other team members to feel comfortable and they will also develop mutual respect and build relationships. Decision making and problem solving are also important skills for high-performing teams to hold each other and the organization accountable for success.

6.10 Rewards and Motivation

Both direct and indirect compensation promote employee motivation and have a positive impact on the high-performance teams. The intrinsic motivators like job satisfaction and encouragement have the highest impact on the performance. Similarly, extrinsic motivators like salary, compensation, and company stocks have an impact on the performance but intrinsic motivators have a better influence.

6.11 Leadership and Communication

High-performing leaders heavily influence their work teams to become high-performing teams. The winning leadership quality which includes the focus on purpose, vision, and values of the organization. Leaders build the commitment and confidence among their teams and ensure that executive leadership team members are constantly involved in challenging projects and honing their leadership skills. Leadership team manages the external customer relationships and focuses on removing the roadblocks that may affect the organization's performance. Similarly, conflict management is an integral part of high-performance leadership and the team. Open communication and focus on coaching the teams instead of directing is appreciated by high-performance teams. The key is to keep communication open to motivate superior performance, keep employees interested, and promote collaboration.

6.12 Empowering Teams

Empowered employees take ownership of their performance and work teams provide opportunities to develop new ideas and facilitate outcome focused decision making. When employees are empowered to make their own decisions, they are more likely to strive hard and perform better to accomplish their tasks. Given the importance of team-based approach in today's economy, there are some common types of teams like work teams, parallel teams, virtual teams, project teams, or leadership teams.

Human Resource Management practices influence through various channels to create and sustain high-performance teams. Companies can be strengthened by leveraging differences in diversity and inclusion. Also, surveys have a positive impact on high-performance teams with diverse individual team members. Diverse workgroups have a high impact on the productivity and innovation of the organizations. Organizations who manage diversity effectively create a value-added advantage for their customers and partners. HR helps to create High-Performance Work Systems by selecting the right mix of talent with the right skills and abilities.

Quiz

1. **Which of the following is not a characteristic of a high-performing team?**

   a. Mutual trust

   b. Communication

   c. Collaboration

   d. Animosity

2. **Organizations try to maintain sustainability, meet _____, and deal with the impacts of globalization.**

   a. clients

   b. politicians

   c. directors

   d. business needs

3. **High-performing teams embrace change and foster creativity.**

   a. True

   b. False

4. For some people, it can be challenging to trust others and
_____ for the benefit of the group.

   a. compromise

   b. compare

   c. contrast

   d. correlate

5. Team members must learn to trust each other, collaborate,
and _____ to deliver impressive results.

   a. travel

   b. innovate

   c. be wary

   d. transfer

6. High-performing teams need _____ members.

   a. talented

   b. abrupt

   c. rash

   d. nervous

7. Teams are inspired by leaders who guide them with _____ and _____.

   a. recognition, shrewdness

   b. salary, journey

   c. trust, hindrance

   d. focus, purpose

8. Empowering teams means _____, _____, _____.

   a. trust, resources, time

   b. supervision, solutions, micromanagement

   c. domination, oversight, control

   d. regulate, manipulate, administer

9. Although it takes time to become an effective team the time is saved in the long term through increased _____.

   a. efficiency

   b. effervescence

   c. errors

   d. elections

10. Leaders build team _____ and _____.

   a. commitment, confidence

   b. adversity, apathy

   c. problems, proximity

   d. laziness, lucidity

Answers	1 – d	2 – d	3 – a	4 – a	5 – b
	6 – a	7 – d	8 – a	9 – a	10 – a

Chapter Summary

Effective leadership increases team dynamics and companies invest time and resources to ensure they have stable, high-performing teams. Organizations try to maintain sustainability, meet business needs, and deal with the impacts of globalization. Teamwork is vital to achieving these goals. Companies explore new ways to engage and motivate employees and improve team performance to achieve higher levels of success. Organizations cannot succeed with one person so it is important to build a strong team culture. Some people are hesitant to embrace working in teams. It is challenging to trust others and compromise for the benefit of the group. Team members must learn to trust each other to best collaborate, innovate, and deliver impressive results. Accountability, transparency, and clear expectations help organizations outperform their competitors. Human resource management practices can help in many ways including managing talent, assisting in conflict resolution, and cultivating diversity and inclusion cultures. One of the strengths of a team is individual differences in skills and ideas that can complement each other. This makes it more likely that a team will overcome obstacles because someone in the team will have an idea and the rest of the team has the energy to complete the challenge. High-Performance teams are a combination of talent, skills, abilities, purpose and goals, leadership, communication, accountability, and responsibility. These teams work toward a common goal for organizational success. High-performing teams need talented team members. Teams of talented individuals make great organizations.

Compensation--both direct and indirect--is the most powerful motivator for most employees. Job satisfaction and recognition are encouraging as well. Teams are inspired by high-performing leaders who guide them with focus and purpose. Trusting teams to make their own decisions and solve their own problems empowers them to succeed efficiently.

Chapter 7

High-Performance Job Designs

Successful organizations have a good strategy,
communicate it to the employees, and empower
them to work toward achieving it. Great organizations
align their goals with their overall market strategy.
Effective human resources departments help to get the
best employees, motivate them to perform well, effectively
measure performance, and retain them through competitive
compensation packages. High-performance work systems
help organizations exel by increasing efficiency, coordination,
etc.

What will be covered in this chapter

- Job design

- Talent acquisition

- Training and development

- Performance measurement

- Compensation management

- Employee empowerment

- High-performance work systems (HPWS)

- The role of HR in high-performance job designs and work systems

- The role of technology in high-performing organizations

- Aligning goals with business strategy

- Performance management in HPWS

- The Impact of high-performance work systems

Employees are the most important and expensive asset for any organization. It is vital for the companies to leverage this asset to create competitive advantage in the market. Human Resource Management highlights the importance of efficient workforces achieving organizational excellence. Many industries have efficient and high-performance work systems with committed workforces; in these industries, employees achieve greater productivity and organizations improve their bottom line.

High-performance work is one of the human resource management systems that focuses on employee involvement and organizational commitment. High-performance organizational performance has two dimensions of work systems: job designs and high-involvement management. The organization increases employee involvement and this has a positive result on the outcome and performance. High-Performance Work Systems

(HPWS) is an effective management practice that creates a work environment within an organization which supports an employee to reach greater efficiencies by giving them higher responsibility and involvement. Designing a High-Performance Work System is about putting all the human elements at the workplace together in order to achieve greater employee potential. A High Performance Work System is all about understanding the key priorities of the organization, designing the jobs to meet the relevance, identifying and attracting the right talent to fulfill the job, and then evaluating the performance of the employee and planning the appropriate compensation to retain the high-performing talent.

7.1 The Value of High-Performing Work Systems

Workforces who are highly involved and committed to the organization's performance, in designing and implementing the workplace policies and processes, are more engaged and perform better in the long run. Many manufacturing organizations using high-performance work systems had a competitive advantage with high labor productivity and efficiency. When employees have the right skills and knowledge and have the power to make the right decisions regarding their performance, they can leverage the company's financial information like costs and revenues, and they are more likely to be engaged and productive. High-Performance Work Systems are interconnected with human resource policies and practices in different HR dimensions like Organizational Development, Talent Acquisition, Performance Management, Compensation & Benefits, and Training & Development. These dimensions play a vital role in improving the employee skills, engagement, abilities, motivation, and growth opportunities

Figure 7.1	Human Resource Practices for High-Performance Work Systems

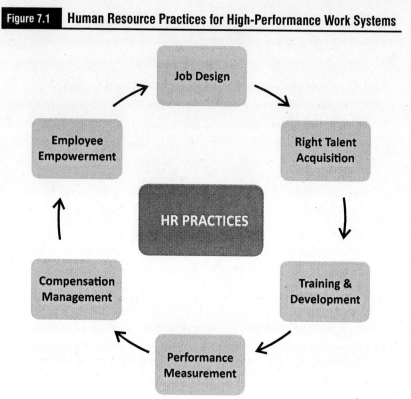

7.2 High-Performance Work Systems and Employee Empowerment

Workers' attitudes and behaviors are limited by their level of empowerment in the workplace. Employee empowerment is an intrinsic motivational approach where employees are empowered to make key decisions about their job performance. Strong and efficient organization competencies are reflected in the self-confidence of the employees. High-performance work systems have a significant impact on an employee's working environment. It is the way of describing the freedom of choosing the way employees can perform their tasks at their own discretion. If employees are empowered to make decisions about their own job performance, they have more potential to react positively to the changing organizational situation and are more likely to be fulfilled about their individual outcomes.

7.3 Role of Human Resources in High-Performance Job Designs and Work Systems

For decades, Human Resource Management has focused on improving employee productivity at different organizational levels. Companies always struggled to create motivated employees and create bottom line impact at the same time. Many companies have different organizational development practices in place to keep the workforce motivated and productive; however, the priority question has remained about the direct impact of the employee motivation and the organization's profitability. Efficient Human Resource practices enhance employee skills and abilities to deal with ongoing organizational change management strategies. Human Resources in a broader perspective improves the way of adopting high-performance work systems practices in all different industry organizations since it entails a unique and faster approach to achieve competitive advantage. HPWS increases the participation opportunities for employees to be involved at various levels in the organization, ultimately improving job satisfaction and leading to a greater organizational commitment.

There are several direct and indirect drivers that affect the workplace performance:

7.4 Technology in High-Performance Organizations

Many organizations are implementing new technologies and systems that impact the work performance of employees. New and greater adoption of technical systems are making the job much easier, however we need skilled and efficient workforces to be able to manage and work with these systems. New IT systems are automated and enable high productivity and are empowering.

7.5 Align Goals with Business Strategy

Whether businesses want to improve their organizational cultures or gain a competitive advantage, management has to align organizational goals with the overall business strategy. Companies in profitable industries are more likely to adapt to the high-performance work system culture and performance management. Companies in more volatile markets are more resistant to this approach and to change any of the compensation systems. Adapting to the high-performance work systems and modifying current reward systems may negatively impact, and is correlated to, unionization in some industries. Firms who are pursuing a differentiation in their business strategy within their markets are more likely to adopt high-performance work systems than the firms who are pursuing cost strategy or vertical expansion. External factors such as market competitiveness have more impact on reward management factors than others.

7.6 Performance Management in HPWS

Employee skills, abilities, and performance management correlate in high-performance work systems. Improved IT systems, performance evaluations, and data gathering on employee engagement, attitudes ensure that human resources professionals can drive performance improvements. It is imperative that organizations are focused on hiring the right talent with the skills and abilities focused on creating future talents required for sustainability and profitability.

7.7 Impact of High-Performance Work Systems

Organizations adopting high-performance work systems have seen long term performance impact on customers, stakeholders, employees, and innovation. HPWS is perceived to successfully affect the firm's profitability and turnover. And HPWS have been an increasingly important source of competitive advantage in today's volatile and changing globalization. Human Resource Management practices are even more important with HPWS organizations such as talent management, talent acquisition, learning and development, performance management and motivation, and employee engagement. Additionally, organizational culture is considered as organizational capital for the sustainable competitive advantage. Strategic change and leadership decisions shape the employee commitment and organization's interaction with external stakeholders.

Effective talent management is an extremely important practice for today's organizations; and companies use HPWS values to attract and retain the high-performing talent for achieving their high-performance strategies. It is crucial for organizations to emphasize the individual goals and career ambitions as part of the talent retention and to make them feel inclusive in the organization's values and strategy. These organizational values are reflected in the attitudes of the management in their day to day tasks and key decisions. They are embedded into the organization's value system which may become the driving force behind positive organizational performance.

Quiz

1. **What does HPWS stand for?**

   a. High-Performance Work System

   b. Harry Potter Will Survive

   c. Hewlett Packard Warehouse System

   d. Highly Proficient Work Standard

2. **To an organization, its human resources are _____.**

   a. its land

   b. its buildings

   c. its employees

   d. its software

3. **Allowing employees to participate in the design and implementation of organizational policies and processes _____.**

   a. is better than a cost of living raise

   b. increases engagement and buy in

   c. has no effect on the organization

   d. replaces the need for motivation

4. A HPWS understands organizational priorities, designs appropriate jobs, fills them with the right employee, and offers appropriate ____.

   a. condolences

   b. candor

   c. collation

   d. compensation

5. Empowerment allows employees the ____ to make choices and trust they will make good ____.

   a. freedom, fortune

   b. desire, drawings

   c. health, hires

   d. discretion, decisions

6. ____ allows employees greater freedom to handle inevitable changes with less stress.

   a. empowerment

   b. challenge

   c. virtue

   d. compensation

7. **Organizations must balance employee productivity and motivation with profits and _____.**

   a. choices

   b. challenges

   c. results

   d. restitution

8. **Technology changes and so must _____ ability.**

   a. employee

   b. decision

   c. choice

   d. condition

9. **_____ and willingness to try new methods of employee motivation and compensation are often linked.**

   a. location

   b. size

   c. climate

   d. profitability

10. Companies with smaller margins are often resistant to making changes that could _____ what little profit they count on.

   a. increase

   b. double

   c. jeopardize

   d. swell

Answers	1 – a	2 – c	3 – b	4 – d	5 – d
	6 – a	7 – c	8 – a	9 – d	10 – c

Chapter Summary

Employees (human resources) are the most important part of an organization. A high-performance work system (HPWS) understands organizational priorities, designs appropriate jobs, fills them with the right employee, and offers appropriate compensation. Allowing them to participate in the design and implementation of policies and processes increases engagement and performance. Organizations that have HPWS have higher productivity and efficiency. Empowerment allows employees the discretion to make choices and trust they will make good decisions. This allows employees greater freedom to handle inevitable changes that occur and that additional freedom decreases stress. Organizations must balance employee productivity and motivation with profits and results. Technology changes and so must employee ability. Profitability and willingness to try new methods of employee motivation and compensation are often linked. Companies with smaller margins are often resistant to making changes that could jeopardize what little profit they count on. HPWS helps companies succeed in the current globalized market.

This page is intentionally left blank

Chapter 8

Information and Communication

Information gathering and sharing ideas is a large part of organizational success. Without effective communication throughout all levels, the organization will struggle to accomplish even the most basic tasks. It is important to focus on improving communication and sharing information more efficiently. Too much information tends to overwhelm employees who do not know which parts are most important. This could lead to an employee or team focusing on the wrong information and completing tasks already completed by others or working on something that the organization no longer values such as an old product that will be discontinued soon. Too little information leads to some of the same problems. Without any guidance or understanding of the bigger picture, employees and teams will have to create goals according to what limited information they have. This could lead to completed tasks that do not align with the vision of executive leadership, the customers, or the shareholders; this is at best a waste of time, and at worst detrimental to the company, its reputation, or a big waste of money.

What will be covered in this chapter

- The importance of information and communication

- Methods of communication within organizations

- Communication within groups and teams

- Communication between groups and teams

Working in teams is one of the key factors of success in business. It highlights the key elements of teams that capitalizes on trust as one crucial building block. The high-performing groups need skilled & talented employees with constant trust-based cooperation among themselves. Trust supports cooperative behavior of top-level teams and also emphasizes the position of trust when constructing high-performing teams. The conceptual approach was high-performing teams' perspectives on trust within organizations. A theoretical framework is proposed via analyzing key characteristics and defining high-performing teams and related concepts. The framework highlights clear vision, trust, and communication from the top management. Team member skills, motivation and responsibilities must be recognized by the leadership. Leadership is a critical component that includes clear roles, standards, and goals.

Teams are the spine of any business and effectively-led groups are trained and can resolve complex business problems, make sound decisions, and utilize creativity and innovation. Teams are the new frontier for workforces and innovation. Leadership and teamwork go hand in hand. It is crucial that leaders of these groups are the role models and teachers, not taskmasters. The leader is central to the success or failure of a team. In today's globalized economy, companies are focused on improving productivity, creativity, and problem solving. The younger generation of employees want to be assimilated differently into the workforce and share their ideas to receptive management. A high performing team is the ideal vehicle to supply this new technology the scope to address the challenges that face all companies now, from internal to external competitors. The past twenty years have introduced a new way humans work together. Companies have striven to trade the interpersonal relationships of their workplaces. They have considered the productivity benefits that teams can carry to the work environment. Now, companies are on the threshold of taking teamwork to the next level. High performing teams can accomplish much more due to the fact they have the backing of the organization and consequently are provided with the tools to make them better achievers.

Many organizations have the possibility to enforce high performing teams inside their work environments. Companies focus on building skills like problem solving, innovation and productivity in order to boost motivation among teams. Companies must consider their corporate culture as it presently stands, market competitiveness in which the organization is operating, and any obstacles that the company may anticipate in short term and long-term business trends. Once these are addressed, any company has the possibility to effortlessly take advantage of high-performing teams.

Most work-related conglomerates of humans fall into the "group" category. A group is defined as humans that are certain collectively with the aid of the truth that they work for the equal company or the identical department. The group is not successful based totally on the crew output if there is not any joint collaboration within the team. The team is made up of high-performing individuals who uplift their team with their skills and talent.

Now that groups have been defined, it is important to understand why a corporation would want to use high-performing teams. High-performing groups have the unique capability to engage all stages of personnel in an employer and make them active participants in the decision making process. By growing a team, companies are making the most of their workforce. Teams are creative and employees need the suitable environment to exhibit their creativity. Teamwork emphasizes trust and creativity and harnesses the team to come up with fantastic options. The difference between high-performing and low-performing teams is the team structure more than the capabilities of its members. One frequent attribute of a low-performing crew is a lack of clearly-defined outcomes. Ambiguous comments or lack of clarity can cause serious problems for the team. Another attribute is a low willingness, participation, and input. Once team members start feeling that their views are not important, it can be quite challenging to align the team again with its usual purpose. The effort that is put into the structure, roles, duties, and expectations of the team participants for the duration of the formation of a team, the greater the likelihood that the group will be a high-performing team.

8.1 Communication Within Organization

Teamwork is a concept that has gained attention lately in the workplace. Last decade showed an increase in the use of teamwork in the place of work; however, recently companies have started to identify ways of improving the functionality of the groups in order to transform them into high-performing teams. This mind-set shift with the focus of creativity and innovation drives steadiness and the long-term sustainability of the company. For the growth of the organization, leaders must emerge as inspirational and innovative. Shifting the mindset from individual work to team-based work took time because of the generational differences that manifest in a place with a varied workforce. A greater recent change in the corporate attitude is to not only to include groups into the working environment, but to supply them with the tools required to be high-performing and successful. Some latest adjustments in technology have additionally allowed teams to attain that high-performing level. For example, agencies have often distributed newsletters or some different form of communication to employees, however with the growing popularity of social media, corporations have the opportunity to further open the lines of communication.

8.2 Groups and Teams

Small to medium sized businesses benefit from using teams. Smaller companies have smaller workforces and that demands that workforces must work together and fulfill many exclusive roles within the company, whereas a larger body of workers may work on simply focusing on the employee's job and keep away from placing the workforce together as a team. This gives smaller groups an advantage of high-performing teams. However, this poses a challenge as well due to the fact that the disadvantage for the company is higher with a smaller worker base. If the team fails in a small company, there would possibly be a larger impact on the company than such a failure would have in a larger company. High-performing groups follow certain key principles that make them successful. While the environment may also be conducive to high-performing teams, these principles ought to be applied to make the team successful.

Leaders must have a clear direction consisting of the visions, goals, and measurable metrics by using which the team will operate and be measured against. Direction is developed at the leadership level and they show inspiring leadership to motivate team members to continue with their responsibilities and instill in them the desire to produce excellent work. This demonstrates an unwavering dedication and commitment by team members to the group and to work collectively to achieve desired goals. Dedicated teams can be seen as the perseverance a group has toward achieving its visions and goals.

Similarly, practicing effective communication by means of which two-way information is developed between the team members, leaders, and the organization. Leaders must make decision making autonomy to achieve the excellence within high-performing teams. Autonomy is the ability to put into operation the courses of action that the group decides are most appropriate. Autonomy provides the teams the authority to act without codevelopnstantly requiring higher stage permission to make decisions for the benefit of the team or project. Leaders also play an important role in promoting diversity. A team should be diverse with individuals of all ages, positions, and backgrounds to promote all possible ideas in a group. Additionally, this will also establish respect within the organization. Respect refers to the way that is indispensable for the group to operate within its personal structure. Team members need to exhibit respect for each other, while the leader needs to have the appreciation of the team. It is additionally essential that the enterprise has respect for the team.

It is a vital requirement that the team share the same common goal that they are striving to obtain together. The first step in unifying the group is to have them develop their goals to achieve them. These can be described by the group itself, not necessarily by management. These targets need to be measurable to be able to gauge the performance of the team. Each goal should have some measurable metric so that higher management can determine the team's overall effectiveness and help the team as they create a blueprint for improvement. The objectives should be accompanied with milestones to achieve throughout the project. These are the desired results that are going to measure how the team is progressing toward its goals over time.

Team individuals ought to understand that their function is a piece of the larger picture. While an individual wants to recognize his or her personal role in the team, they also need to be in a position to fill in for others. The group has to sense the accountability to fill others' roles in their absence due to the fact that the crew knows the goal is vital to the employer and achieving success is the final target. A unifying goal lets the team contributors transition between roles and keeps consistency in the performance due to the fact they are working toward the goal, as well as their individual responsibilities. Direction is critical because teams owe their existence to the organization; and goals should be set both for the team and for team members. There need to be standards for evaluating teams or the individuals within the team to maintain accountability. By having unifying desires and objectives, the team feels totally included. High-performing groups have participants that sense they have an important place not solely in the team but in the organization as well. Along with identifying goals and objectives, the crew have to identify precise limitations to success, or any feasible resistance that the team may also face from other participants of the company, as well as external barriers. These must be outlined and mentioned so that the team is conscious of issues that may additionally come up and mutually create solutions to overcome them.

Quiz

1. **Without trust team members hesitate to share _____ for fear of ridicule.**

   a. information and ideas

   b. money

   c. health advice

   d. parking spaces

2. **Leaders should be role models and teachers, not _____.**

   a. supportive

   b. taskmasters

   c. encouraging

   d. helpful

3. **Global companies focus on improving _____, _____, and _____.**

   a. discipline, intimidation, oversight

   b. micromanagement, etiquette, prejudice

   c. productivity, creativity, problem solving

   d. difficulties, stress, encouragement

4. **The younger generation of employees wants to _____ more than their older peers.**

    a. work

    b. relax

    c. collaborate

    d. drive

5. **Which of these does not improve team motivation?**

    a. Innovation

    b. Productivity

    c. Micromanagement

    d. Problem solving

6. **What should good team members do?**

    a. Point out every fault of their team members

    b. Argue about every idea introduced

    c. Put the group above themselves

    d. Talk to HR about minor disagreements

7. **Team creativity can be explored in buildings, but can also be worked on in _____.**

    a. virtual communications such as video conferences

    b. solitude with nobody around

    c. isolation with only one member of the team

    d. noisy public places

8. Low willingness to participate and offer input leads to team
   _____.

   a. success

   b. motivation

   c. difficulties

   d. excellence

9. Effective teams have _____.

   a. difficulty deciding who should be responsible for which duties

   b. clearly defined roles

   c. hourly meetings about minor decisions

   d. strict, constant oversight from a manager

10. Newer organizations are more likely to communicate through _____ than _____.

    a. printed newsletter, social media

    b. electronic newsletter, printed newsletter

    c. newspaper, tweet

    d. fax, email

Answers	1 – a	2 – b	3 – c	4 – c	5 – c
	6 – c	7 – a	8 – c	9 – b	10 – b

Chapter Summary

Trust is the building block of teams. Without trust, team members hesitate to share information for fear of ridicule or communicate openly afraid of losing a competitive edge over a coworker. Good leadership is important to team success. Leaders should be role models and teachers, not taskmasters. Global companies focus on improving productivity, creativity, and problem solving. The younger generation of employees wants to collaborate more than their older peers. Companies value the productivity benefits of teamwork. Companies focus on employee improvement like problem solving, innovation, and productivity, which boosts team motivation. Teams are groups of individuals working toward a common goal and trusting each other to put the group above themselves. Teams are creative and need space to explore that creativity. This collaboration usually happens in a physical building, but it can also happen through virtual communications such as video conference meetings. Teams flounder when there is low willingness to participate and offer input. Clearly defined roles for each team member is necessary to an effective team. In the past decade, companies have tried to make groups into high-performing teams. Shifting organizational mindsets from individual-based work to team-based work took time because of generational differences. Organizations have changed with the times and technology and communication is less likely to be a printed newsletter and more likely to be electronic or social media communication. Small businesses are less likely to be separated into silos and more likely to communicate with each other in team-based ways even without considering themselves an official team. Small businesses often have better teamwork, but if the team fails, so does the company. Large businesses are more siloed, but if one of the many teams fails, the impact to the overall organization is much less devastating. Leaders need to clearly communicate their vision and direction so teams can more effectively pursue organizational goals. Autonomy of teams is very important to efficiency. Teams need to be able to make decisions on the best way forward and act on those decisions while leaders trust them to do the right thing. Diversity of team members increases diversity of ideas, skills, and attitudes, which increases the team's ability to overcome unforeseen obstacles. Ideally, there is respect between team members, between teams, and between the organization and the teams. It is important for the team to be striving toward the same goal. The goal should be measurable with a clear impact on the organization. Teams should be allowed to make goals within these parameters and leaders should trust teams to make decisions that improve the company. Diverse team members with unique qualities strengthen a team, but some overlap is essential in case a team member is absent. Cross training or knowing each other's duties can help in such cases. Individuals and teams should set goals that align with the organization. Teams should think about possible challenges, limitations, or barriers externally or within the organization. This will help them overcome the obstacles when they arise.

This page is intentionally left blank

Chapter 9

Power and Politics

Power comes in different forms including physical, psychological, structural, political, and economic. One form of structural power is supervisory positions that have the permission from the organization to oversee, assign tasks, evaluate, reward, punish, and terminate an employee. This form of power is the most impactful. Other forms of power include reputation (both positive and negative), charisma, rationality, and enthusiasm. Employees have power when they act together. If all employees on a team object to abusive or inappropriate behavior from their supervisor, then have the power to raise concerns to human resources, upper-level management, executive leadership, government agencies, or even the press. This power in solidarity usually keeps most supervisors in check, but not always. Office politics is the term used to describe the different ways employees, supervisors, teams, departments, divisions, and executives align or oppose each other and their ideas and goals.

What will be covered in this chapter

- Different ways organizations use power

- Power at all levels

- Power and leadership

All organizations are unique within their culture and leadership. Although the changes in leadership may additionally be unique, the power and political culture in companies are often quite similar. Power and politics are the lifeblood of most organizations, and, as a result, the managers support power dynamics; but they should also understand the impact on the teams. Companies are composed of coalitions and alliances of exceptional parties that continuously compete for accessible resources. A major impact on how decisions are made is the distribution of power amongst the leaders. Unequal distribution of power in organizations can have a fundamental effect on culture, employee engagement, market competency, employee motivation, job satisfaction, absenteeism and turnover, and stress. Therefore an awareness of the strength and authority is integral for a higher understanding of these other behavioral processes. Power is usually associated with authority and leadership, but it comes from other places as well. On individual or work team levels, many individuals try to have an impact in groups by using power tactics. A wide variety of mechanisms are available to neutralize the attempts and knowledge of these strategies supports a manager in managing his team. In summary, strength and political methods in organizations signify and affect the culture of the companies. A leader's verbal ability, decision-making, power, and politics can notably have an impact on the behavior and the attitudes of employees. The concept of power and politics is closely associated with authority, leadership and managing. Power is informal authority.

9.1 Different Ways Organizations Use Power

As stated above, many different methods of power are useful to managers. But there are some ways organizations use power and politics.

9.1.1 Controlling Access

Most choices rest on the availability of applicable information, so leaders controlling the access to information plays an essential function in the decisions made. One example of this is the common practice of labeling certain facts as corporate confidential information. Similarly, another tactic is the practice of controlling the right of entry to respective individuals within the organization.

Additionally, very few organizational decisions ought to be made concerning the most suitable standards for evaluating results. As such, significant power can be exercised via those who can practice selective use of objective criteria that will lead to a decision

Few would argue that the most profitable and effective groups are those that continuously pursue excellence. This striving starts with the top leadership of the organization. However, leaders do not now command excellence, they build excellence. Excellence is doing everything you can within the bounds of doing what is proper for your organization. If excellence starts off evolving with leadership, then that leader should be of a good character. A leader's character shapes the tradition of his or her organization and consequently the public opinion of the organization.

If leaders are to inspire others, they must have a clear sense of their professional values. These values will be distinct to every leader, and they should be honestly evident to everyone in the organization. Leaders must trust in the values they express, and must work difficult to get their private values in sync with these of the organization. People appreciably admire leaders who understand where they stand on important standards and have self assurance in their personal beliefs and values. Ultimately, the successful organization will find out and embrace shared values. Leadership is also about building relationships and adding value to others. Relationships both add to, and subtract from, an individual's life. Leaders will both have either a high quality or poor influence on their followers, but they will certainly have an impact. Leaders with robust positive character will pursue making matters better for those that comply with them, which leads to building an excessive degree of mutual trust. Ineffective and weak leaders can effortlessly damage their organization, and it has been demonstrated that it is easier to affect an organization's culture.

9.2 Power at all Levels

Key resources of organizations are people and material resources. Human Resources of the business works on changing or converting the people assets of the enterprise in the skills needed to be able to produce finished or consumable products. In an attempt to transform the critical assets of the organization, choices must be made to use current resources efficiently in order to achieve the desired product or outcome. Sometimes it is necessary to use power or politics while making decisions. Thus, the impact of politics in corporations and using politics to get things done is normal. In any organization, we use human assets for support. This calls for the inevitability of organizational power and politics. The organizational relationship is the political action and encompasses the most troubles underlying organizational politics. A leader's strength is best used to make the right decisions for the company, employees, and community. Sometimes power plays or other attempts to use power for selfish purposes backfires and is rejected. In this case, it does not influence anyone as the perpetrator had hoped. If leaders want to successfully influence others, they should consider individuals, groups, and situations when making a decision.

Possibly the most common influential tactic is rational persuasion. This involves using facts, data, and logical arguments to influence others. It is most effective when the persuader is also an expert or has a solid grasp of the technical knowledge and the surrounding market conditions of the organization.

Another major way to influence with power is to share what you have as a leader. Psychologically, most people feel a sense of giving back when they are provided with favors. Leaders who give favor to others can usually expect others to do favors for them in return. Leaders additionally influence others by first demonstrating it with their personal actions.

Leaders develop allies. Reciprocity is also necessary in developing networks of allies, people who can assist a leader accomplish his or her goals. Leaders can influence others by means of taking the time to discuss with followers and other leaders to recognize their desires and concerns. Leaders seek advice from other leaders and can amplify their network of allies to accomplish goals. Some leaders make their networks bigger through hiring, transfer, and promotion processes. Identifying and retention programs for key positions supports organizations to employ individuals who work together on the preferred outcomes and help achieve goals.

9.3 Power and Leadership

Charismatic people often become natural leaders or are viewed as leaders so their influence is greater than an average employee. Charismatic leaders can create a compelling vision and help drive goals to completion. Charisma is usually considered a personality trait, but it can also be a skill that is improved with careful practice.

Quiz

1. Organizations may be different, but office politics _____.

   a. is always the best way to get things done

   b. are exactly like governmental politics with elections

   c. are often the same wherever you go

   d. should never be used to get things done

2. Employees often form informal alliances and compete for _____ resources.

   a. available

   b. delicious

   c. real estate

   d. human

3. Power distribution among leaders can affect power dynamic among the rest of the _____.

   a. leaders

   b. stockholders

   c. board of directors

   d. employees

4. **Individuals often use _____ to influence others or accomplish things.**

   a. baked goods

   b. threats

   c. power tactics

   d. money

5. **Controlling access to information _____.**

   a. is one way to control who has power

   b. is the job of the ceo

   c. should be left to new employees

   d. means giving information to everyone at all times

6. **How _____ is used in companies greatly affects the organizational culture.**

   a. email

   b. parking

   c. software

   d. power

7. **Leaders with integrity _____.**

   a. gain the respect of their employees

   b. lose the respect of their employees

   c. gain weight in office competitions

   d. lose weight in office competitions

8. **Leaders who act in the best interest of others will improve all their lives and earn an unparalleled level of _____ and _____.**

   a. health, fitness

   b. profit, loss

   c. trust, respect

   d. office space, parking spots

9. **If a leader is an expert, a good way to persuade others is through _____, _____, and _____.**

   a. kindness, gifts, threats

   b. shouting, direct eye contact, pointing out mistakes

   c. time off, luxurious chairs, cruel emails

   d. logic, facts, data

10. **Demonstrating the desired conduct often encourages others to _____.**

   a. lead

   b. follow

   c. retreat

   d. attack

Answers	1 – c	2 – a	3 – d	4 – c	5 – a
	6 – d	7 – a	8 – c	9 – d	10 – b

Chapter Summary

Organizations may all be different, but power and office politics is usually the same wherever you go. Employees often form informal alliances and compete for available resources. Power distribution among leaders can affect power dynamics among the rest of the employees. Power imbalances fundamentally change an organization in many ways. The effects reach employee culture, engagement, motivation, satisfaction, absenteeism, turnover, and stress. Individuals often use power tactics to influence others or accomplish things. How power is used in companies greatly affects the organizational culture. Power can be seen as informal authority. Controlling access to information is one way people in organizations maintain and control who has power. Controlling access to physical areas within the organization is a physical way to use power to exclude certain individuals or groups. Leaders who control the early phases of starting an organization have a much stronger influence on the corporate culture; and how the employees behave affects how the public views the company. This means leaders should carefully calculate how they want to use their power within the organization because of the tremendous influence they have. Leaders with integrity gain the respect of their employees. Leaders who act in the best interest of others will improve all their lives and earn an unparalleled level of trust and respect. Sometimes the easiest way to get something done is through office politics. Another way to get things done is to persuade others through logic, facts, and data. It helps to be an expert in the field to quickly earn and maintain credibility and influence. Cooperation is another form of influence. Doing favors for others often drives them to return favors or at least consider the ideas of the giver. Reciprocity can build networks of allies and people who can help. Demonstrating the desired conduct often encourages others to follow without having to be persuaded.

This page is intentionally left blank

Chapter **10**

Decision Making, Conflict, and Negotiation

People make decisions many times every day. Some are unimportant, but others are monumental. People communicate every day. Effective communication is a skill that is well worth the time and effort required to master it. Motivation is a broad topic, but this chapter will cover it along with accountability. In an organization keeping employees motivated while also tracking their progress to hold them accountable is a balance that leaders must get right. Building positive relationships is a good principle in life because it makes potential allies out of strangers and coworkers. It also lays a foundation for effective teamwork.

What will be covered in this chapter

- Decision making

- Leadership

- Communication

- Motivation

- Accountability

- Building positive relationships

Several times we come across the conflicts with our workgroups, coworkers, family, etc. This not only creates tension but also at times turns into escalation especially when emotions are involved. It is extremely important for professionals in the workplace to understand conflict management because conflicts can be mentally and emotionally draining. There is no way to avoid conflict. Therefore, it is vital to understand these emotions and learn to deal with them effectively without jeopardizing the relationships.

Conflicts can have positive outcomes as well. Organizations are training their workforces to encourage healthy conflicts as it can support new ideas and innovations. Many times, conflicts are the outcomes of negotiations. Organizational leaders can support negotiations and healthy conflicts by using more of a positive and productive approach. Healthy negotiations with conflicts can actually bring productive outcomes. If leaders are trained on effective negotiation tactics, it can not only support the overall organization at all levels and benefit from it. It is therefore vital to manage conflicts by keeping emotions in check and not letting conflicts suppress emotions and jeopardize the work relationships. Leaders frequently come across power struggles internally and externally with partners, customers, etc. It is imperative that leaders understand the power struggles that they may come across during their professional lives.

Work Teams and groups in global organizations are becoming crucial and more prominent with less positional power and authority. They are becoming more independent and less dependent on positional power, eventually becoming less dependent on the direction from authority. Teamwork in organizations is proven highly effective while working with diverse teams. Diverse teams give perspectives to key decisions at various levels within organizations. However, where there is diversity, there are also conflicts. Therefore, leaders also have to manage and train their workforces on conflict management skills. Understanding and applying effective conflict management skills can lead to many positive outcomes with the teams. Additionally, understanding the negotiation best practices and effective conflict management will help develop the basic skills that leaders require for professional success.

Frequently, when team views differ and are not able to reach a reasonable solution, both the parties will work on exaggerating their case in a best possible way. Conversely, team members will only follow teams who follow the perspectives that resonate with their own. Leaders with positive attitudes require aptitudes to act in the time of emergency and to arrive at an effective resolution, especially in this globalized economy.

Teams that are not able to resolve conflicts or differences in an effective manner due to poor negotiation abilities usually encounter issues in achieving their target, goals and delivering high quality results. This ultimately affects customers, partners, and employee satisfaction. When key projects are delayed and tasks are not completed as planned for achieving business objectives, it negatively affects the organization's credibility.

10.1 Decision Making Leadership

Leaders have a prominent role in an organization. Internal and external stakeholders look to the leaders for making key decisions for the business and people. When we think about a leader, we envision someone who is decisive and certain. If leaders are not clear and certain about the decisions they make, it is difficult for various stakeholders to trust the leader. A leader must be able to communicate goals and decisions clearly and concisely to the business.

Leaders often have to make challenging and difficult decisions which affect customers, partners, employees, etc., therefore they have to ensure the decisions made are data driven and were carefully considered before they were made. Great leaders understand how to balance emotions while making difficult decisions that positively impact themselves while supporting their customers, partners, and employees.

Organizations understand the value of high-performing teams and high-performing leadership. This is why the organizations value the importance of the leadership and work teams to achieve business goals. Team building remains as tough as ever and strong visionary leadership helps teams to shape the culture of organizations. Businesses often represent different products, services, and promotions and unsurprisingly teams have to work in diverse cultures. There is no question that teamwork is a key factor to the success of any organization. Therefore, it is important that leaders must cultivate high-performing teams and also effectively lead them.

10.2 Communication

Leaders set a benchmark for communication in organizations. Teams cannot perform effectively without clear communication. Additionally, it is the leader's responsibility to develop a clear communication benchmark within companies to work toward business goals. Some people are very responsive to the facts and if the leaders do not communicate clearly; it not only demoralizes the workforce but also retention will become difficult. Some individuals are more receptive to passion and convictions so it is important for leaders to communicate with enthusiasm.

A high-performing leader clearly communicates the purpose and values and members are mutually responsible and accountable for outcomes. Employees are committed to achieving business outcomes with purpose, vision, trust, and common values of the company. When teams are empowered in decision making, employees of a high-performing team will be involved and understand the purpose of their goals and objectives. A team will be more empowered if the team understands the parameters and goals of key business objectives. If the decisions, accountability, and expectations are clearly defined, it helps high-performing teams to take responsibility and self-manage.

Leading effective teams has been challenging for the leaders including employees with low engagement and misalignment in this volatile and uncertain business environment. High-performing teams focus on clearly communicating, aligning with their team, getting buy-in, and creating extreme accountability. High-performing organizations believe in creating leaders at every level.

10.3 Motivation and Accountability

It is a leader's responsibility to be able to motivate high-performing team members and to have the ability to act to get others motivated to work toward their desired goal. They also need to be able to influence employees to generate the outcomes through collaborating with diverse teams and cultures that support achieving desired goals. A leader must be able to keep the commitments and model the desired behavior, cultivate appropriate cultural values, and regularly acknowledge great outcomes. Similarly, when a leader establishes commitment within their teams, it fosters positivity and empowers teams on achieving results by accountability culture.

10.4 Building Positive Relationships

Employees grow and develop themselves if they are challenged with accountability. Leaders are seen as a mentor and coach in organizations. Therefore, they are seen as building positive relationships internally and externally to build and nurture high-performance teams with positivity, integrity, and trust. Additionally, with the bias for action that is required in high velocity uncertain times, a leader with high trust is better able to make sound decisions for business and people.

Leading with the authority includes not only making decisions for a department, business unit or organization, but also it is imperative for leaders to be proficient at negotiation skills with effective decision making. The decisions made in day to day business directly affect partners, employees, and customers. Making rational and logical decisions are the key attributes for leaders to ensure that organizational and ethical decisions are made with the legal and political frameworks in mind. Leaders also use their wisdom to learn from the decisions that were not successful. They not only influence but also energize and mobilize the internal stakeholders based on the market demands. Leadership is often challenged to make decisions with less data available in these uncertain market conditions and turbulent times. During these ambiguous times, leadership relies on teams to get the information, data, and research needed to make decisions. In dynamic times and ever-changing technological landscapes, leaders and organizations step up to follow the data driven decision approach to avoid ambiguous decisions.

Similar to decision making, negotiation is an imperative part of a leader's lives. Organizational leaders at all levels negotiate very often on various decisions made. Therefore, understanding and managing the negotiation discussions in key decisions is an effective way to accomplish goals and win the deals. These business decisions empower the workforces to develop themselves and improve their work environment. Teams work on difficult issues and projects to keep the project moving forward that the leader has set for them.

Quiz

1. **Conflict is _____.**

   a. unavoidable in most cases

   b. never a good thing

   c. personal attacks

   d. clear and concise

2. **One source of _____ is misunderstanding.**

   a. trust

   b. synergy

   c. conflict

   d. praise

3. **Conflict is a good thing if _____.**

   a. you love to argue

   b. it is handled properly

   c. you are the leader of a large organization

   d. people quit

4. **Encouraging respectful disagreement can lead to creative _____ and _____.**

   a. insults, arguments

   b. solutions, innovations

   c. problem solving, absenteeism

   d. nothing, nowhere

5. **Teaching employees how to handle conflict allows teams to _____.**

   a. disagree and quit

   b. heighten emotions

   c. manage themselves

   d. form larger teams

6. **Team members should leave their emotions behind and focus on _____.**

   a. the ways to achieve the goal

   b. exaggeration

   c. distrust

   d. persuasion

7. **With emotions removed from the equation, it is easier to see that disagreements are not _____.**

    a. a personal attack

    b. a defense

    c. people

    d. organizations

8. **Leaders should communicate _____ whenever possible for maximum persuasion.**

    a. loudly

    b. quietly

    c. enthusiastically

    d. horribly

9. **Leaders should _____.**

    a. set a good example through their actions

    b. scream and shout to get their point across

    c. wave their arms and pound their fists for emphasis

    d. make as much money as they can without regard for the company, employees, or surrounding community

10. **Leaders are seen as mentors and coaches in many organizations and they are responsible for building teams with _____, _____, and _____.**

   a. clever gimmicks, short cuts, disregard for others

   b. enthusiasm, ruthlessness, killer instinct

   c. technical savvy, selfishness, arrogance

   d. positivity, integrity, and trust

Answers	1 – a	2 – c	3 – b	4 – b	5 – c
	6 – a	7 – a	8 – c	9 – a	10 – d

Chapter Summary

Conflict is unavoidable in the long run. Sometimes it can be avoided for a short time, but conflict is all around us every day. One source of conflict is misunderstanding the desires of others. Communication is vital to resolving conflict while preserving important and necessary relationships. Conflict can be a good thing if handled properly. People often fail to imagine other points of view and encouraging respectful disagreement can lead to creative solutions and innovations. Making sure conflict is managed properly requires a skilled leader. Teaching employees how to handle conflict is a good exercise. This allows teams to manage themselves while rarely needing intervention from an authority figure. One way to effectively handle conflict is to remind individuals that the goal should be to focus on the task at hand and leave emotions out of it. If team members can leave their emotions behind and maintain focus on the goal, it becomes clear that disagreements are not personal and a disagreement should not be viewed as a personal attack. Leaders should be clear and concise about their decisions and direction for people to go. This requires excellent communication. Leaders should make sure decisions are based on data rather than opinion. Leaders should cultivate effective team attitudes. When details are readily available a leader must take extra precaution to communicate clearly without eggateration or alteration of the facts. Leaders should communicate enthusiastically whenever possible for maximum persuasion. Setting a good example is a powerful motivator. DISH Network CEO is a billionaire, but he goes to work at 9:00am every day and climbs the stairs to his 4th-floor office carrying his home-made lunch. This has a clear impact on employees in that facility. Leaders are seen as mentors and coaches in many organizations and they are responsible for building teams with positivity, integrity, and trust.

This page is intentionally left blank

Chapter 11

Basic Attributes of Organizations

Organizations often share similar attributes. While organizations generally try to present themselves as unique, there are certain characteristics shared among most organizations. Organizations are made up of people grouped into teams around common goals. Leadership sets a certain tone that permeates throughout the organization and often this tone is enforced by terminating people who do not comply. This is usually what is meant by organizational culture. Organizations have demands imposed by customers or shareholders or regulators. To meet these demands, tasks with deadlines are assigned to capable employees.

What will be covered in this chapter

- Leadership roles and skills

- Organizational global culture

- Organizational environment

- Managing workplace stress

- Leadership fundamentals

- Emerging perspectives

Organizational culture affects how employees behave in a given situation. Many organizations use HR policies and practices as a key factor to change the culture, employee behaviors, and how it can be managed effectively. Organizational culture is a set of values and beliefs that organization portrays and attitudes of the employees in which they behave and accomplish the tasks. Culture has a significant impact on retaining the high-performing talent and also attracting the talent providing the competitive advantage. Additionally, culture has a key impact on people's behavior. The values and norms that have formed the culture by the visionary leaders of the organizations on how to behave and what to expect from the organizations. The process of creating the culture is characterized by the way organizations behave and treat their employees. The values of the organizations play an important role in building the culture. The values are expressed in many different ways within an organization - like how the management cares about their people, how the competencies are built in a company, the market competitiveness, if the organization is customer focused or internal focused, the innovation and quality, and the collaboration of the teams within a company. Top management in any organization must understand organizational behavior and work-related behaviors of their teams. Additionally, managers should work toward motivating employees, resolving conflicts, and supporting employees to set goals to achieve performance excellence. Leaders who understand the employee behavior are in a better position to shape the culture and improve the decision-making capabilities. Understanding the employee's attitudes, individual differences, and embracing the diversity can help the leadership teams to collaborate and shape the global cultures. Organizational culture also helps the way companies interact with customers, vendors, partners, competition, political environments, etc.

11.1 Different Leadership Role and Skills

Leadership includes the process of working together with others to achieve organizational objectives in a competitive marketplace. High-performing leadership has many responsibilities to accept a changing environment and form a high-performing culture. Usually leadership functions consist of planning, organizing, leading, and controlling. The leaders have the responsibility of environmental scanning, budgeting, organizational and so on as it is the integrating force for all organizational activities. When employees work together to accomplish a common goal, they organize themselves to achieve optimized results. The business enterprises not only monitor costs and revenues in their financial books but also shape the culture by creating motivational programs that attract employees.

11.2 Organizational Global Culture

Expectations of the customers are changing rapidly, and organizations must be ready to adapt to the customer needs in a quickly changing environment. The expectations and pressure of stakeholders can be challenging and rewarding for leadership at the same time. The efficiency of the organization is greatly influenced by the employee behavior. Even the most automated and high-technology organizations have the human asset as the most integral part of their organization. Companies interact with customers, partners, vendors, suppliers, employees, and job applicants and different forms of communication are required to work with different parties. In order to be effective, leadership must view every individual as a different and unique opportunity to improve on the organizational behavior and culture. The behavior of employees and groups build the expectations of the culture within an organization. Certain roles and responsibilities within an organization have a strong impact on the individual behavior and individual behaviors have a stronger impact on the organization culture. Companies learn to manage individuals and teams by way of managing behavior of individuals, organization structure, job design and processes. An organization's typical structure is about how its employees and teams are formed and how it is structured on their organizational chart. The communication, processes, leadership decisions and organizational design are some of the examples of processes within an organization. At times, when a process or organization structure fails, this will result in reviewing the entire organization structure and will help to redefine the structure to optimize efficiencies.

Cultures have a positive or negative impact in organizations. A positive culture will help in improving the efficiency, productivity, and motivation of the company; whereas a negative culture will create hostile situations, bring more lawsuits, and disrupt the productivity and morale of the company. Leadership must pay attention to the structure, processes, and culture to improve the efficiencies, productivity by developing the skills to identify the issues early on. Issues like negative customer feedback, increasing employee absenteeism, decline in profitability, etc., direct the leadership to look into the culture of the company. Leaders have to adapt to different roles to be able to accomplish organizational goals. When leaders are able to apply their Knowledge and experience to adapt to the given situation, they can work toward solving critical business problems. Managers often make decisions based on their intuition rather than facts and data, and therefore it may create favoritism toward certain team members. Managers are able to make better decisions if they rely on facts rather than intuition, setting goals for the team using SMART methodology, or setting up structured interviews with benchmarking scores as part of the hiring process. The SMART methodology means a goal is specific, measurable, achievable, relevant, and time-bound. To be effective and efficient, managers must be able to apply the knowledge, competencies, and skills to their interpersonal competence while dealing with employees.

11.3 Organizational Environment and Motivation

With the impact of digitalization and global boundaries, these organizations and leadership must be responsive to the changing situation. Every company must be able to respond effectively to changing political constraints, economic and technological environmental changes, and foster a culture of innovation within the organization. Leadership who are able to respond quickly to changing organizational demands are able to gain the trust of their teams and support the positive culture within the teams. Increased government regulations have affected the organizational decisions and employment practices, leadership must adapt to these changes to find innovative ways to motivate their teams.

The organization's performance depends on the individual and team's performance. If managers are able to manage cultural diversity, attitudes, perceptions, values, and individual expectations, then employees will be motivated to interact at a higher level that will positively impact performance. Management often uses the reward systems to increase employee's performance and these reward systems can also act as the perks to attract and retain the skilled talent.

Managers work on developing teams to accomplish company's goals. If managers effectively recognize the individual's contribution, it will positively impact the performance of that employee and encourage others within the team to do the same. As the teams interact with each other, they develop unique characteristics like processes, roles, rules, etc., which creates its own unique culture. This is why every team has its own unique culture. Additionally, every manager has to learn to manage conflicts including intra-team conflicts. It is important to note that too much of intra-team conflict can lead to the competition and impacts the culture negatively.

Leadership greatly influences employee's performance and motivation. Atmosphere that encourages and supports improvement and innovation plays an important role in the motivation of the individuals. When managers are sensitive and focused on competencies, skills, and ability, it may all positively affect the employee's productivity. If managers fail to understand the needs, goals, and preferences of the individual team member, they may miss many opportunities to positively motivate the employee.

11.4 Managing Workplace Stress

Work-life balance and work stress are not new topics for the organizations. Many companies work on improving work-life balance for employees so they can effectively manage work stress. Issues such as conflicts at the workplace, technology issues, project deadlines, strained relationship with the manager, financial stability of the company, mergers and acquisitions, change management, etc., all can put tremendous stress on the employee. Stress adversely affects the employee behavior, productivity, performance, and that stress spills over to the employee's personal life, which in turn affects the entire community. With the rapidly changing environment and technological advancement, it is impossible to control stress, but organizations can certainly come up with the initiatives that can help employees to manage the stress effectively. High levels of stress will impact morale and satisfaction and decrease productivity which ultimately impact the bottom line and profitability. Stress is different for different people and every individual manages stress differently; therefore, it is important for organizations to come up with initiatives that are unique and adaptable. There are many organizational stressors, but politics continue to be a source of primary stress in many organizations. Company politics, power play and struggles can create friction and competition among people within a company and increase stress.

Organizational culture, lack of feedback, lack of growth, downsizing can create stress among the employees. Like individuals, every company is unique and has different personalities. Top executives and leadership of the company shapes its distinct culture. Employees want to have regular feedback on their performance. If managers are able to provide regular, timely feedback, it can provide a meaningful impact on the employees. Performance feedback is a way organizations can minimize stress and opens a two-way communication for managers and employees.

11.5 Leadership: Fundamentals and Emerging Perspectives

Strong leadership is the most integral part of any organization. It not only shapes the organization's culture, but also affects the motivation and performance of the employees and eventually affects the bottom-line profitability. Leaders are the change agents of the company, and their attitude and beliefs greatly influence the organization's goals. Effective leaders must be able to deal with individual teams that positively impact the organization's goal. Leadership efficiency and effectiveness is typically measured by 360-degree performance evaluations that include feedback and surveys with their team members. Similarly, leadership and power go hand in hand. Power includes the ability to get things done in a way that one wants. With leadership comes authority and power. Many managers use a high degree of power to accomplish their goals; however, if power is used in a wrong way it can ruin the relationship with the teammates ultimately affecting the culture.

Employee-focused leaders focus on supporting employees in the best way to accomplish company goals while also considering employee's personal development. Employee-focused leaders are concerned and supportive of employee's personal advancements, growth, and achievement. Some leaders emphasize individual development with the expectation of effective work performance. Ability to influence followers is one of the key factors of the leaders. Leadership traits such as use of power and influence over followers result in the effectiveness of the physical, sociological, and psychological traits. Some leaders use a situational approach initiating structure and emphasizing the importance of collaborative work within the teams. The leaders' knowledge and skills are needed to evaluate the problem, make quality decisions, and need the support of the teams to implement the decisions. Leadership is a complex process and leaders assess, adapt, and formulate goals and vision of the organizations. Articulating a vision and building and reinforcing a commitment, a leader builds a charismatic profile and transactional leadership involves engaging the followers with meaningful objectives to achieve business results.

Quiz

1. SMART goals are _____, _____, achievable, _____, and time-bound.

   a. specific, marketable, respectable

   b. scientific, motivational, responsible

   c. successful, manageable, relatable

   d. specific, measurable, relevant

2. Companies like Google spend time and money cultivating and maintaining a specific culture because _____.

   a. they have lots of money

   b. organizational culture greatly impacts employee retention

   c. employees formed a union

   d. it is cheaper than hiring robots

3. HR policies affect organizational culture by dictating _____ and _____ behaviors.

   a. happy and sad

   b. high and low

   c. inner and outer

   d. acceptable and unacceptable

4. Organizational structure is important and must be reviewed and corrected when it becomes _____ or _____.

   a. inefficient, ineffective

   b. inappropriate, inspirational

   c. informative, improper

   d. independent, insulting

5. It can be viewed as favoritism when leaders act on _____ rather than _____.

   a. stability, support

   b. intuition, data

   c. facts, rumors

   d. opportunity, foresight

6. _____ can improve individual and team performance in many ways by managing attitudes, perceptions, values, expectations, etc.

   a. regulations

   b. markets

   c. taxes

   d. managers

7. **Great managers _____ and _____ impressive individual results.**

   a. recognize, reward

   b. punish, prohibit

   c. forbid, forget

   d. study, correct

8. **If leaders are sensitive to the needs and abilities of each team member, they can _____.**

   a. use this knowledge to manipulate employees

   b. seize opportunities to motivate employees

   c. decline help from other leaders

   d. make their own jobs easier

9. **Many companies work to reduce _____ to maximize attendance and effectiveness.**

   a. light

   b. noise

   c. food

   d. stress

10. _____ **leaders support individual career development.**

   a. employee-focused

   b. new-age

   c. old-school

   d. health-conscious

Answers	1 – d	2 – b	3 – d	4 – a	5 – b
	6 – d	7 – a	8 – b	9 – d	10 – a

Chapter Summary

HR policies affect organizational culture by dictating acceptable and unacceptable behaviors. Organizational culture greatly impacts employee retention. That is one reason companies like Google spend so much time and money cultivating and maintaining a specific culture. Often employees, leadership, and HR can be heard talking about whether certain candidates "fit in" at a company or on a specific team. Leaders are responsible for planning and organizing so employees understand important objectives. Organizations must be able to quickly adapt to changing market conditions and customer demands. Organizations impact employee behavior, but the actions of employees impact the organization's culture. Organizational structure is important and must be reviewed and corrected when it becomes inefficient or ineffective. When leaders act on intuition instead of data it can be viewed as favoritism. Leaders must set a good example at all times and remain above reproach. Governmental regulations affect organizational decisions and employment practices. The organization's performance depends on the performance of individuals and teams. Managers can improve individual and team performance in many ways by managing attitudes, perceptions, values, expectations, etc. Great managers recognize impressive individual results and reward them. By doing this, managers can drive team behavior that positively impacts organizational goals. Leaders must be sensitive to the needs and abilities of each team member so they can seize opportunities to motivate employees. Many companies work toward reducing stress on employees to maximize attendance and effectiveness. Employees can be stressed about individual conflicts, deadlines, company stability, technology, office politics, and more. Managers play an important role in minimizing stress on their teams. Leadership effectiveness and efficiency can be measured by 360-degree feedback surveys. Managers often use their power to get things done, but the more they use their power, the greater the chances of abusing it. Leaders should be careful to attempt to achieve goals with as little force as possible. Employee-focused leaders support individual career development, which improves future company leaders and retains talented employees.

This page is intentionally left blank

Chapter **12**

Strategic Competency and Organizational Design

Organizations constantly strive to find better ways to succeed. They work towards improving methods to meet customer demands, motivate employees, and remain profitable.

What will be covered in this chapter

- Effective use of technology
- Organizational design
- Cultivating leadership
- Expanding the talent pool
- Effective training initiatives
- Learning and development
- Change management
- Benefits and compensation

Many organizations are experimenting with work designs to motivate employees to achieve the right balance between work and personal lives. The key factors are the companies who want to attract, retain, motivate, and value the employees in this tight labor market. One of the major key factors of effective job performance is the job design. Job designs are when the organizations clarify what they want each employee to work on. The success of any company depends on the business processes and the structure. The organizations use the expertise and the knowledge of employees to create a competitive advantage in the marketplace. Objectives of the organizations are to optimize the business, use the skills of the employees, and produce new competitive products and services to sustain a competitive advantage. One of the biggest challenges for the organizations is the ability to align all the components of the organization to support the ability to compete. As business strategies become more and more complex, leaders have to adapt to the changing environment, and they must be able to inspire and guide the teams. Leaders who understand how to make good, sound business decisions will need robust data and diagnosis of the SWOT of the topic. A SWOT is a way of evaluating the strengths, weaknesses, opportunities, and threats that face an organization or department. Strengths and weaknesses are the positive and negative attributes within the organization. Opportunities and threats are factors that affect the organization from the outside. This can be upcoming regulations or relaxed restrictions, two rivals merging, a new technology being invented, etc. Additionally, they need to have the involvement strategy to ensure the decisions made engage key stakeholders, conceptual business frameworks and the disciplined management approach to implement and execute the decision. Business strategies and organizational design are more complex with the changing technological instabilities. Guiding through significant change and organization design with the objective of building new and developing current employees may be the most important and complex objectives of human resource professionals. It not only requires a trusted relationship with senior management but also the deep knowledge of the business and ability to drive human resource initiatives with the eye on the business impact. Talent acquisition, organization design, learning and development, change management, and total rewards programs are some of the critical examples that keep human resources busy.

12.1 Technology Supports Technology

Organizational designs are more than just the organizational structures. Today's leadership understands the importance of the effectiveness of the organizational capabilities to compete in market space. But many lack clarity around this topic and how to create an efficient organizational design. The question is how to align the core components of the business to execute the strategy and create a competitive advantage. Leadership must be able to remove barriers so employees can make the right and timely business decisions. As businesses are becoming more complex, leaders have the responsibility to be able to do more than just inspire their teams. They will need to analyze and understand the complexity of the organization. To be able to make sound organizational decisions, leaders must have to have a robust diagnosis of the business issues and the opportunities that it entails. The strategy is to ensure the involvement of key stakeholders and disciplined project management to turn the decisions into action. Businesses are more complex than ever, not only due to global expansion and competing with local competitors. Ever changing business models and management of the business portfolio of different business models are the key to the business effectiveness. Companies who are able to manage the multidimensional organizational designs are able to gain competitive advantage over the firms that are not able to change with the market dynamics. Guiding a leader and manager through an organizational design with the objective of building new skills and capabilities is not only important for today but also especially important to align with the vision of the organization. Human resource professionals have an important responsibility of building deep and trusting relationships with the business to understand and act accordingly.

Supporting the strategy of the organization is the key objective of the organizational design. Business and technological disruptions often threaten organizational sustainability and few businesses recognize the internal barriers to control and align with the external factors. Companies can alter a few factors that affect them, but they can certainly control the way companies can deal with these forces. The core principle of organizational agility is helping the global organizations to strike a balance of sustainability and market competitiveness. Companies increase their agility to serve customer demands. Ultimately, these principles of organizational agility are supported from technological advancements, powerful strategy, and matrix projects environments to fulfill business requirements.

12.2 Organizational Design and Talent Pool

Organizational design should start with the purpose, values, and vision to understand how it sets them apart from their competition. Once organizations have identified the key unique selling proposition that separates them from the competition, it gives a sense of purpose to the business. Companies who are able to create a sense of purpose, are able to clearly articulate the purpose and values to the employees. Leadership may have to set a bold direction and a forward-focused culture is crucial. For many companies, organizational design initiatives fail due to poor communication from leadership to the individual contributors within an organization. When companies are setting up the new organizational design programs, the organizational structures should be considered last, not first. In the past, the reorganizations were always focused solely on the structure, without understanding the business strategy and involvement of the leaders. Fast growing globalization and technological advancements have created new business models that helped leaders to understand the organizational factors that slowed the response in the past.

Attracting and retaining the top talent is crucial for businesses. Leadership assumes that the current talent personalities and capabilities do not affect the design of the organization, but they do. To make the most of the talent available, it is critical for companies to design positions that use the strengths of the employees in their positions. Companies must understand the technical skills and manage the business acumen of the employees while making sure that leaders are equipped to foster the collaboration and empowerment. Companies must ensure that there is a connection between the skills and capabilities for the leadership talent. Key competencies of the employees and organizations predict the performance and add a competitive advantage to the business. Traditionally, companies have focused on technical skills but building business agility requires broadening the portfolio to include other core competencies and preparing for disruptions with technology and business. Leadership is required to communicate the mission, purpose, and change to its employees so they can prepare for the dynamics and make timely decisions to execute the strategy that impacts the profitability of the business. This requires often engaging and partnering with geographically diverse teams. Organizations are evolving everyday around ever-changing customer demands and working on fulfilling those demands. Organizations are becoming more agile in decision-making and have viewed outsourcing as the key to control costs. The enterprises when they develop business strategy to support the visions, mission of the company and powerful IT strategy. Today more and more businesses are realizing the importance of the powerful infrastructure to support the future organizations.

12.3 Cultivate Leadership

Senior leaders of highly agile organizations play a very integral role in building cohesive, clear, actionable systems that focus on priorities and results. The dynamic global business environments often alter the perspective and focus of the leadership and management. Decision making must be available at all levels and is no longer reserved for the top managers. As the real-time situation changes, the business steadily makes decisions about the higher complexity of the market. This also requires leaders who can anticipate and understand the importance of making the right decision at the right time. Not only leadership must support and identify active leaders who are driven about the business, industry, and customers. The process of performance management must be able to evaluate and identify emerging new leaders. With the increasingly complex and changing business environments, the bar of leadership is raised in the last decade which requires different traits in today's leaders including designing new processes, evaluating and understanding people's behaviors, eliminating the obstacles to productivity, leading change management, and balancing internal and external factors impact on overall organization. To be able to manage the complex and disruptive business environment, leaders must accept the process-oriented management vision and values. Organizational structures should be designed to manage the automation and technology changes. Continuous process improvements must drive measurements to facilitate continuous improvements and drive the performance results and profitability.

12.4 Elevate Training Initiatives

Over the past decade, global organizations have been continually evolving. For companies to remain competitive, they need to invest in learning and development programs that prepare employees for the future. The learning objectives must align with the organization's vision to develop their workforces in order to remain competitive. An increasingly changing landscape and rising complexity are reshaping business expectations and skills required to meet these expectations. It is important for companies to look carefully into their learning initiatives and align those with the business vision. The digital shift is creating a vibrant workforce and exceptional leaders; however it is also important to understand the behavior and expectations of the employees while creating these programs.

Quiz

---

1. **What does SWOT stand for?**

   a. Saved without overt turmoil

   b. Shown withstanding other trials

   c. Strengths, weaknesses, opportunities, threats

   d. Success while others try

2. **Many organizations are experimenting with ways to motivate employees to have a good _____ balance.**

   a. speed-quality

   b. cost-speed

   c. quality-cost

   d. work-life

3. **Leaders must be able to inspire their teams in a constantly _____ environment.**

   a. improving

   b. changing

   c. declining

   d. crushing

4. Understanding the characteristics of the organization and its competition allows companies to survive and _____.

   a. thrive

   b. fail

   c. squander

   d. operate

5. A useful _____ department is busy with talent acquisition, organizational design, learning and development, change management, and rewards programs.

   a. maintenance

   b. finance

   c. shipping

   d. human resources

6. Leaders should use their power and influence to _____ that prevent their team members from succeeding.

   a. build walls

   b. develop silos

   c. remove barriers

   d. harass people

7. **Leaders in complex organizations need to not only inspire their teams, but also _____.**

   a. understand how their team impacts the organization

   b. buy treats every day to add more motivation

   c. have daily meetings to discuss long-term goals

   d. make sure their teams do not get too lazy

8. **Businesses should find a unique angle that separates them from their _____.**

   a. money

   b. competition

   c. ideas

   d. goals

9. **Strengths and weaknesses are internal organizational characteristics, while opportunities and threats _____.**

   a. are important to think about

   b. describe the organization in great detail

   c. are helpful to contemplate

   d. describe the marketplace outside the organization

10. When decisions must be made at higher levels every time _____.

    a. customers get fast service

    b. employees give fast service

    c. customers wait longer for the company to act

    d. employees enjoy unresponsive management

Answers	1 – c	2 – d	3 – b	4 – a	5 – d
	6 – c	7 – a	8 – b	9 – d	10 – c

Chapter Summary

Many organizations are experimenting with ways to motivate employees to have a good work-life balance. A company must use its expertise and the knowledge of its employees to create and maintain a competitive advantage in the marketplace. Leaders must be able to inspire their teams in the face of a constantly changing environment. Understanding the characteristics of the organization and the competition allows companies to survive and thrive. A useful human resources department is busy with talent acquisition, organizational design, learning and development, change management, and rewards programs. Leaders should use their power and influence to remove barriers that prevent their team members from succeeding. As organizations become more complex, leaders need to do more than inspire their teams. Leaders need to understand the characteristics of the organization and how their team fits in. This allows them to guide their team more effectively. Disruptions from businesses and technology impact organizational stability and sustainability. Few businesses accurately recognize internal factors that must change to best adapt to external forces. Businesses should find a unique angle that separates them from their competition. This will help them build a brand identity and will help customers distinguish between brands. When conditions change quickly, it is important for decisions to be made from lower levels of the organization. This is where the company interacts with customers so this is where the needs are first discovered and where the final decision is implemented. If the decision must go to higher levels of the organization and wait for approval or new direction, the customer must also wait. This provides a negative customer experience and is one of the disadvantages of organizational structures requiring multiple layers and extended time when a decision is needed. Organizations should strive for constant improvements that drive results and profitability. Companies invest time and money into learning and development programs to remain competitive.

Chapter 13

High-Performance Organizational Cultures

This chapter discusses high-performance cultures and organizations, how to create a high-performance culture, how to go from a vision to performance, and traits of high-performance work teams.

What will be covered in this chapter

- Leadership is crucial to organizational success.

- Leaders should be familiar with market conditions.

- Leaders should align organizational goals to meet market conditions.

- Company culture, process, systems, and structure should align with market conditions.

- High-performance work teams share certain characteristics including goals, talent, skills, purpose, motivation, leadership, and empowerment.

Every company has a different culture and some managers
are better able to cope with this difference and can manage
their team in a different culture. Some cultures of organizations
can more effectively enhance performance and productivity.
Managers have a big impact on how they shape the cultures of the
companies and the way they manage to enhance the performance
and productivity of their teams, which leads to every company
having a unique culture. Members at different levels of
organizations agree on the values of the company as a whole. For
the companies in every sector, they are focused on the long-term
performance and looking for different ways to outperform the
competition. Usually, in high-performance organizations, people
are energized and positive. They are confident and proud about
the projects they are working on. Employees have clear roles
and responsibilities of the tasks and they own their tasks. When
companies take a strategic approach toward becoming a high-
performing organization, they understand organizational and
people capabilities that drive profitable results. Organizational
culture is an approach that has become an important concept in
the business field. The fundamentals of the organization's culture
sets the foundation of attitudes, beliefs, and behaviors within a
company. In every company there are various types of people
with different behaviors and attitudes. The ability to bring these
attitudes to work together to achieve a common goal is the key
to the company culture. There are many variables that need to
be considered while understanding the ideal work setting in an
organization. When team members work together and collaborate
with each other to achieve the desired goal, they believe in certain
values which are common to others in a group. Organizations
form the groups in order to achieve the desired outcome which a
company has targeted. Often culture emerges from the vision of
the organization and represents the guidelines to the structure and
processes. When the employees have an opportunity to contribute

to the vision and mission of the company, the culture becomes a high-performance culture.

The effectiveness of an organization is measured by its ability to grow and sustain its competitiveness in the market. This exemplifies organizational competence. Organizational competence is the study of the company's ability to sustain the high-performance culture capable of delivering quality products and services over time. It helps to provide insights into how the company's values are aligned with people values and behaviors. When the organization is able to sustain the quality of its products and services to its long-term growth, it is able to attain the trust of its people and sustain high-performance learning culture.

However, it is easier said than done; sometimes the senior leadership of a company does not understand the marketplace in which the organization competes. Most of the time, it leads to a vision, mission, and strategy that are either misleading or unclear. When leaders have an inaccurate understanding of the company's mission and vision, it gives unclear direction to its people and leads to a different understanding and different culture. As a result, the company's culture, processes, systems, and structure may not be aligned with the marketplace expectations. If the behaviors required to successfully implement the business strategies are out of alignment with customer and market requirements, it can often lead to dissatisfied customers. This can in turn affect the culture of the company and employee behaviors. Such issues are typically a variance of the behaviors required to create high-performance sustainable culture. The high-performance culture must focus on empowering employees, responsiveness, and accountability at all levels within an organization.

Additionally, organizational systems and infrastructure often fail to support the company vision and strategy. As a result, the company spends too much time on internal issues and politics rather than external factors such as customers and market competitiveness.

13.1 Creating a High-Performance Culture

Responding to the marketplace, employee behaviors are the key to create high-performance cultures. When all the factors including leadership, marketplace, employee empowerment, systems and structures come together in the right combination, it creates a culture that has a competitive edge and is able to generate impressive results. The study of the company's ability to build and sustain a culture that is capable of delivering high-value results over time for its customers, creates a culture that is capable of high-performance. Cultures evolve over time and serve as a guiding principle to the company values. It is up to leaders to define and shape this culture. The sustainable organization remains responsive to market changes and expectations to adapt and align with customer expectations.

High-performance organizations focus on building key strategic skills of the organizations. The leaders are trained in the many areas such as team building, strategic planning and management, financial impact, efficient project management, managing team performance, forecasting industry trends, etc.

Change management is delicate. Most people do not like change so they resist it without thinking about it very much. It is extremely critical for organizations to initiate the change among the employees. The awareness of the changes at this level is an important factor. Many leaders fail to communicate the upcoming changes in a timely manner to the organization and that leads to ambiguity and speculation. The leadership team should be supportive in overcoming the resistance to changes and support the organization's collaborations in their work. High-performance organizations and leadership embrace change and communicate this change effectively to the companies. They not only plan strategically but also effectively manage their teams during this change. Open and ongoing communication between the management and leadership help support the change and overcome resistance.

13.2 From Vision to Performance

When companies attempt to implement organizational change with an unclear strategy, often the organizational change management fails. Organizations need competent leaders now more than ever. Competent leadership and their vision help recognize the key issues and strategies to mitigate those issues. Employees at all levels within the organization must have the visibility and transparency of the company strategy. Moreover, the employees must be empowered to make key strategic decisions within their work area. Many would say their best associations are those that try to continually strive for greatness. This striving begins with the top management of the organization. However, a key point to note is that leaders build the excellence that is expected from the workforce. In the event that greatness starts with authority, at that point that leader must be of a good character. A leader's character shapes the way of life of their workforce. People cannot be respected leaders if they lack integrity in their personal lives. Employees will not be able to trust someone who has major character flaws. If it is obvious that the followers are getting inconsistent or mixed messages, then at that point it is essential for a leader to improve his personal life and work toward the organization's success and gain the trust of the employees. Leadership character is additionally about building key connections and boosting employee's confidence and self-esteem. These relationships either add to or take away from an individual's life. Leaders will either have a positive or a negative effect on their peers and followers. They will definitely have an effect. Leaders with positive influence have a strong impact on their teams.

13.3 Traits of High-Performance Work Teams

There is no simple recipe to create a high-performance work team and effective groups. Every team has unique characteristics. There is a shared understanding of what makes an effective team. High-performance work teams usually have similar characteristics and are composed of various combinations of goals, talent, skills, purpose, motivation, leadership, empowerment, and other standards. High-performance teams are the work teams that operate toward accomplishing a common goal or objective. They are often committed to working with each other. Team members in these teams do a great job when their roles are clear. They are skilled in their jobs and also understand the underlying reason behind every task they do. Every member clearly understands and supports the common purpose of the team and overall organization. Therefore, clarifying the purpose and connecting it to every employee's role within the company enhances the team's potential and motivates the team members to stretch themselves to achieve their goals.

High-performing organizations begin by evaluating the effectiveness of their recruitment and retention programs. They begin by recruiting and retaining their most talented employees, while helping their low performing members to find other places to work. Morale typically in these organizations is extremely high and it increases as the performance increases. After selecting the right talent, it is important to ensure that the team possesses the right skills including decision making and interpersonal skills. Employees must also show commitment toward performance excellence, respect, conflict management and so on. Additionally, organizations must hold employees responsible and accountable for the tasks they perform.

Companies come up with different creative ideas for incentivizing high-performing teams. Both monetary and non-monetary rewards that encourage high-performing employees have a positive impact on their performance and accomplishment of their goals. Usually intrinsic rewards such as work satisfaction and interesting projects work well for long term reward systems. Additionally, believing in an employee's abilities encourages them to achieve team goals by taking more strategic risks.

Quiz

1. Members of every level of the organization should _____ on company values.

   a. disagree

   b. agree

   c. argue

   d. debate

2. High-performance organizations tend to have employees who _____.

   a. argue with managers, debate with coworkers, and dispute data

   b. bring their own food to work to save the company money

   c. show pride in their work, have clear roles, and show initiative

   d. park far away from the building to walk more steps each day

3. _____ includes a company's ability to deliver high quality products and sustain that success over the long term.

   a. company confidence

   b. business bravado

   c. organizational competence

   d. situational stereotypes

4. **If senior leadership fails to understand the surrounding marketplace the company's culture, processes, systems, and structure may not be aligned with _____.**

   a. marketplace expectations

   b. customer confidence

   c. stock performance

   d. press releases

5. **Successful leaders are trained in areas such as _____, _____, strategic planning, financial impact, and forecasting industry trends.**

   a. hypnosis, astrology

   b. diversity, divisiveness

   c. team building, project management

   d. inclusion, instability

6. **What is one of the most important parts of change management?**

   a. financial stability

   b. loyal customer base

   c. high stock prices

   d. clear communication

7. **Leaders who lack personal integrity are _____.**

   a. the best kind of leaders

   b. not well respected

   c. able to get more done

   d. always talking about their crimes

8. **High-performance work teams usually share characteristics like _____.**

   a. speed, intensity, quality, quantity, determination, prejudice

   b. charisma, defensiveness, decisiveness, sloth, hesitancy

   c. attitudes, strategy, operation, structures, fracturing

   d. goals, skills, purpose, motivation, leadership, and empowerment

9. **In high-performance organizations people are _____ and _____.**

   a. energized, positive

   b. stubborn, ignorant

   c. forgiving, anxious

   d. strong willed, selfish

10. High-performance teams work toward accomplishing a common ____.

   a. product

   b. cold

   c. office

   d. goal

Answers	1 – b	2 – c	3 – c	4 – a	5 – c
	6 – d	7 – b	8 – d	9 – a	10 – d

Chapter Summary

Members of every level of the organization should agree on company values. This shared vision helps guide decisions at all levels in a way that benefits the company. High-performance organizations tend to have employees who show pride in their work, have clear roles and responsibilities, and show initiative. Companies succeed when they bring people with different attitudes and skills together and allow them the opportunity to work toward a common goal. Organizational competence includes a company's ability to deliver high quality products and sustain that success over the long term. It is important for senior leadership to understand the marketplace surrounding the organization. If not, the company's culture, processes, systems, and structure may not be aligned with marketplace expectations. This leads to unhappy customers. Companies are most successful when they balance the right combination of leadership, employee empowerment, systems and structures, and marketplace knowledge. Successful leaders are trained in areas such as team building, project management, strategic planning, financial impact, and forecasting industry trends. Clear communication from leadership is one of the most crucial parts of change management. It is important for employees to understand the company vision. Leaders show their character through their actions and this affects their teams. Leaders who lack personal integrity are not respected. It is important for leaders to positively influence their teams. High-performance work teams usually share combinations of characteristics like goals, talent, skills, purpose, motivation, leadership, and empowerment. High-performing organizations recruit and retain highly talented individuals and as the organization succeeds employee morale improves.

This page is intentionally left blank

Chapter **14**

Change

Companies of any size, within any industry, are struggling with the constantly changing marketplace. Political, economic, sociocultural, technological, environmental, legislative (PESTEL), and competitive factors create increased complexities for organizations to execute their mission and deliver against their organizational strategies and objectives. Whether organizations are publicly or privately held, for-profit entities, nonprofit organizations, academic institutions, or governmental agencies, no organization is impervious to change. If you do a Google search on Change Management, the search will return 10.25 billion hits, with common themes around strategy, process, initiatives, and tools. As Benjamin Franklin once stated, "Change is the only constant in life. One's ability to adapt to those changes will determine your success in life." Leaders and organizations must adapt, or the world will pass them by.

What will be covered in this chapter

- The concept of change and change management

- Forces impacting change

- The three types of change and the stakeholders it impacts

- Successful behaviors for organizations to navigate change management

- How to assess an organization's readiness for change

- The concept of an organization's adaptive capacity

14.1 Change Management

Webster's Dictionary defines change as: 1) to make different in some particular; b) to make radically different; and c) to give a different position, course, or direction[1]. It's this last definition that defines change in the marketplace for leaders and organizations to navigate their way into the headwinds of change. The process of change management then is the deliberate, disciplined, and systematic process that deals with transitioning an organization's mission, vision, values, strategy, goals, processes, initiatives, and behaviors toward a new direction to better meet the ever-changing landscape of the marketplace and the organization's customers. The successful discernment of the realities facing an organization, the impact that those headwinds present to the organization, the revision and communication of a new strategy to address these new challenges, or oftentimes opportunities, and the successful implementation and enculturation of change management initiatives is the goal for leaders.

---

1. "Definition of CHANGE," March 15, 2024. https://www.merriam-webster.com.

Change is dynamic. Organizations are organisms. Just as the molecular structure of the body contains DNA, cells, water, proteins, and fats and are housed by connective tissues, muscles, and bones, an organization has people, functions, strategies, processes, products, and services within an organizational structure and culture. Therefore, just like the human body must evolve, organizations must be adaptive to environmental changes by attending to uncertainties, complexities, barriers, as well as opportunities. Being sufficiently mindful and discerning and effectively mobilizing organization strategy and resources to such changes sets up the organization for potential success.

Professor Richard Badham of Macquarie University identifies both formal, overt, and rational forces as well as informal, covert, and non-rational forces that impact organizations. The former is described as an organization's structures and systems and the latter as an organization's culture and politics. The formal, overt, and rational are in response to the PESTEL changes as identified above, while the informal, covert, and non-rational forces are in response to the emotions, diversity of perspectives, and the patterns of politics and power within organizations.

The most common examples of when a change initiative is needed include implementing a new technology, mergers and acquisitions, changes in leadership, changes in organizational culture, or times of crisis. All of these have the potential to impact an organization, so leaning into and planning for change is a way to accommodate the new initiatives within the organizational culture. From here, there are typically three types of change initiatives. They include:

- **Developmental change** – when an organization is looking to improve or optimize its previously established strategies, processes, and organizational structure to support serving its customers.

- **Transitional change** – when an organization is moving away from its current state to solve a problem, such as a merger and acquisition (M&A) or the addition of new technology.

- **Transformational change** – when the change initiative is set to alter the culture, core values, structure, and operations of the organization.

All change is difficult. A recent Forbes article stated that 62% of people do not like to leave their comfort zone or do so only occasionally[2]. Due to this, the change process takes tremendous flexibility, adaptability, and resiliency within organizations and their people.

Prosci is considered one of the leaders in Change Management consulting. They lead change through a people-focused approach to developing an agile, change-ready organization. From this perspective, they see change occurring at three levels:

- **For individuals,** to enable people's success by supporting them through their personal change journey.

- **On a project,** to increase outcomes and return on investment by driving adoption and usage.

- **Across an enterprise,** to deliver strategic intent, mitigate saturation, and improve agility by embedding change management.

---

2. Murphy, Mark. "The Big Reason Why Some People Are Terrified Of Change (While Others Love It)." Forbes. https://www.forbes.com.

This approach is supported by research from Deloitte Insights from their 2023 Human Capital Trends report. In this study of over 10,000 leaders in organizations across 105 countries, it was found that 90% of senior executives consider being more agile as important or very important with two-thirds saying very important. However, only 10% of these same executives see their organizations as highly agile today[3]. While the causes for change in their organizations differ, the amount of change that these organizations will go through over the next few years will have a tremendous impact on their organizational strategy, processes, structure, and ultimately, their people.

14.2 Successful Change – What it Takes

Leaders must constantly align with the market needs and competition and create more resiliency to become more competitive. High-performing and forward-thinking leaders of organizations change rapidly with market demands and focus on delivering the highest quality products and services to customers by adapting to innovation and developing new leaders and teams while ensuring their workforces change rapidly. In other words, organizations require a very resilient and responsive workforce to respond to market demands. Leaders who can consistently manage change and promote process improvements and methodologies across team engagements can fulfill customer demands promptly by rapidly transforming into innovative and changing mindsets.

3. Deloitte Insights. "2024 Global Human Capital Trends." https://www2.deloitte.com/us/en/insights/focus/human-capital-trends.html.

In a survey of nearly 3,000 executives about the success of their organization's transformation efforts, McKinsey discovered the failure rate to be higher than 60%, while Harvard Business Review conducted a study that suggested more than 70% of transformation efforts fail[4]. These are sobering statistics that spend a lot of time, money, and effort, ultimately impacting organizational cultures, which in turn, create all sorts of other issues in terms of employee engagement, job satisfaction, and ultimately, employee attrition.

According to research from the Project Management Institute, organizational change fails for the following reasons[5]:

- 32% due to poor project management skills

- 20% due to a lack of effective communication

- 17% due to unfamiliar scope and improperly defined objectives

- 14% due to an inability to cope with technology

Some of the above are strategic reasons, while others are tactical. However, everything starts with leadership. Poor leadership and a lack of alignment on a vision for change is the beginning of the domino effect for ineffective change management. Not defining goals promptly or not defining the right goals is a catalyst for failure. In addition, not defining the right resources immediately impacts an organization's ability to execute change. This must be accurate and clear before anything is communicated to those that will lead to change or be impacted by

4. Carucci, Ron. "Organizations Can't Change If Leaders Can't Change with Them." *Harvard Business Review*, October 24, 2016. https://hbr.org.

5. Project Management Institute | PMI. Accessed March 20, 2024. https://www.pmi. org/.

it. For those leading change initiatives, having an agile approval process and a clear implementation process with appropriate metrics to measure change is critical to assess performance. Since most people are resistant to change and lack the commitment to execute it, having clear communication as to the "why" change is important, is critical to overcome fear, conflict, and doubts, and ultimately increase adoption and enculturation.

Employees are at the heart of any change initiative. Since change is an ongoing process too, leaders must recognize this and lead accordingly. Change and culture consultancy, Hallio, identifies the following pillars for successful organizational change management[6]:

- C-level executives and managers must be on board

- Clear goals should be set

- The impact of change needs to be understood

- Employees need to embed a change-centric mindset

- Employees' psychological needs must be understood

- Desired employee behaviors should be reinforced using recognition

- Transparent, frequent, and honest communication is a must-have

- Organizational change management requires collaboration and co-creation

- Change efforts should be measured

---

6. Martic, Kristina. "The Ultimate Guide to Organizational Change Management (OCM)." Haiilo, March 10, 2020. https://haiilo.com.

Proper analysis and discernment of the environmental impacts affecting an organization, creating a sense of urgency, clearly communicating a change vision and strategy, and enrolling the appropriate people to lead the change process are critical to the success of any change initiative.

14.3 Assessing Organizational Readiness and Adaptability to Change

Before an organization can adapt to change, it must first assess its organizational readiness for change and understand the impact that this adaptation will have on its people, strategy, structure, and process. Change influences organizational behavior.

Acclaimed professor and business consultant, Juan Carlos Eiccholz offers a compelling analysis of assessing organizational readiness in his book *Adaptive Capacity: How Organizations Can Thrive in a Changing World*. Before an organization can adapt to change, it must first understand its own behaviors. Two criteria that inform an organization's reality include the type of work an organization does (Technical vs. Adaptive) and the environment in which the organization operates (Stable vs. Unstable).

Eiccholz believes that the difference between technical and adaptive work is an organization's learning agility. When faced with technical work, does the organization's behavior tend to do what they already know and what they have always done, as opposed to adaptive work, where the organization's behavior challenges assumptions, paradigms, conventional wisdom, and the status quo to learn something new? The more adaptive the type of work, the more adaptive the organizational behavior will be to manage and implement change.

The world is becoming increasingly unpredictable and dynamic. Leaders must understand the environment in which their organization competes. Is it stable or unstable, with stability being defined as the possible influence and threat that external forces could pose to its operations? There are four types of organizational behaviors based on this model:

- **Communal** – the environment is primarily stable and a larger proportion of the work is adaptive. Examples include unions, religious organizations, academic institutions, political parties, etc. These organizations deliberate on external forces driving change more slowly.

- **Innovative** – the environment is primarily unstable, and a larger proportion of the work is adaptive. Examples include advertising agencies, biotech companies, consulting firms, media companies, etc. These organizations need to resolve problems quickly due to the instability of the environment in which they operate.

- **Bureaucratic** – the environment is primarily stable and a larger proportion of the work is technical. Examples include law firms, hospitals, auditing firms, public transportation, utilities, etc. These organizations are not used to the speed of change due to regulations and governance dictating the stability of their environment.

- **Action-driven** – the environment is primarily unstable and a larger proportion of the work is technical. Examples include the military, banks, hotels, insurance companies, airlines, etc. These organizations must face change rapidly due to the instability of their environment.

| Figure 14.1 | **Juan Carlos Eichholz's Adaptive Capacity** |

Stable **Unstable**

PARTICIPATORY

	COMMUNAL ORGANIZATION **Stable Adaptive**	INNOVATIVE ORGANIZATION **Unstable Adaptive**	
	Stable Technical BUREACRATIC ORGANIZATION	**Unstable Technical** ACTION-DRIVEN ORGANIZATION	

Adaptive (INTERNALLY ORIENTED / EXTERNALLY ORIENTED) **Adaptive**

Technical **Technical**

HIERARCHICAL

Stable **Unstable**

Understanding an organization's natural behavior assists leaders in evaluating its organizational readiness and adaptability to change. Once leaders recognize their organization type, they must then assess the impact of change on five areas of the organization. Compared via the lens of the human body, these include:

- Purpose: Its mission, vision, and core values = the soul.
- Strategy: It's North Star = the brain.
- Structure: Its organizational design, structure, and locus of control = the skeleton.
- Culture: Its beliefs, values, norms, and agility = the lungs.
- People: Their talent, competencies, and levels of engagement = the blood.

There are multiple assessments leaders can use to discern the above within organizational cultures. These include the Adaptive Capacity assessment, the OCAI, and the OCTAPACE. All these assessments get to the heart of organizational behavior and culture.

The Adaptive Capacity Assessment was developed by Juan Carlos Eiccholz in 2014. It is a twenty-five question assessment measuring the five areas above, with five questions per area. In addition to the quantitative questions, assessors are asked to provide specific examples to validate their responses.

The Organizational Culture Assessment Instrument (OCAI) was developed by Kim Cameron and Robert Quinn in 1999. It measures six dimensions of an organization – Dominant Characteristics, Organizational Leadership, Management of Employees, Organizational Glue, Strategic Emphasis, and Criteria for Success.

The OCTAPACE was developed by Udai Pareek in 2007. It is a forty-question assessment that measures eight core areas of organizational culture and behavior – Openness, Confrontation, Trust, Authenticity, Pro-action, Autonomy, Collaboration, and Experimentation.

Organizational behavior is a critical foundation shaped by an organization's culture. It defines how work within an organization gets done and how the infrastructure gets utilized. Organizational behavior reflects cultural values, beliefs, and norms, and is foundational to future success. While there are many other change management assessments and inventories, these are specific to organizational readiness and adaptability to change, while also being empirical and statistically significant. In other words, these assessments offer a great benchmark to understand an organization's adaptive capacity for change before kicking off any change management initiative.

Quiz

1. **Change is constant in organizations.**

   a. True

   b. False

2. **PESTEL stands for:**

   a. Political, Economic, Scientific, Technical, Employees, Legislative

   b. Political, Economic, Sociocultural, Technological, Environmental, Legislative

   c. Process, Environmental, Systematic, Transformation, Employee,

   d. Political, Employee, Systems, Transformation, Environment, Legislative

   e. None of the above

3. **Change impacts for-profit and nonprofit organizations but does not impact academic or governmental organizations.**

   a. True

   b. False

4. **To make different in some particular; to make radically different; to give a different position, course, or direction. These statements define:**

   a. Transformation

   b. Adaptation

   c. Enculturation

   d. Change

   e. None of the above

5. **Organizations can be viewed as organisms.**

   a. True

   b. False

6. **Responses to emotions, diversity of perspectives, and the patterns of politics and power are part of:**

   a. Formal, overt, and rational

   b. Informal, covert, and non-rational

   c. Formal, covert, and rational

   d. Information, overt, non-rational

   e. None of the above

7. **The three types of change are:**

   a. Basic, intermediate, advanced

   b. Easy, moderate, difficult

   c. Developmental, Transitional, Transformational

   d. Adaptive, Flexible, Resilient

8. **Change occurs at what levels within an organization?**

   a. Individuals, partnerships, process

   b. Individuals, projects, performance

   c. Individuals, partnerships, tactics

   d. Individuals, projects, enterprise

9. **According to the 2023 Human Capital Trends report, it was found that _____ of senior executives consider being more agile as important or very important.**

   a. 90%

   b. 67%

   c. 70%

   d. 50%

10. According to McKinsey, the failure rate of organizational transformation efforts is higher than _____, while Harvard Business Review estimates that _____ of transformation efforts fail.

   a. 70% / 70%

   b. 60% / 50%

   c. 60% / 70%

   d. 50% / 60%

Answers	1 – a	2 – b	3 – b	4 – d	5 – a
	6 – b	7 – c	8 – d	9 – a	10 – c

Chapter Summary

The marketplace is dynamic. Competition is constant. Organizations are consistently presented with formal and informal market forces such as political, economic, sociocultural, technological, environmental, legislative (PESTEL), and competitive factors impacting their business as they struggle for survival and growth. Leaders and organizations must keep up and adapt, or their organizations will perish.

Change does not discriminate, and it impacts any organization, of any size, in any industry, whether it be for-profit, nonprofit, academic, or governmental. Leaders must identify headwinds impacting their organizations and navigate their people through change. Leaders play a pivotal role in strategic discernment and effective communication in guiding organizations through the intricate phases of developmental, transitional, or transformational change, each one having its unique impact on the organization and its culture.

Change can be stressful, and the more responsive, resilient, and prepared leaders and their organizations are to implement change management practices, the more successful they will be in leading change as a deliberate and systematic process. The lack of readiness may impact an organization's success in navigating the barriers and pitfalls of effective change.

Fortunately, there are many frameworks, methodologies, and processes to assist leaders in navigating their organizations through change. However, the foundation of any organization and any change management initiative is people. Therefore, to navigate high failure rates, leaders must foster organizational resiliency and cultivate a responsive and adaptable workforce, equipped with good strategy, clear communication, and effective project management. Leaders and organizations must take the same level of care in navigating change as they do in executing an organization's mission and vision or executing its corporate strategy to deliver its goals and objectives.

This page is intentionally left blank

Chapter **15**

Human Resource Management Systems

L arge organizations face a particular issue that smaller organizations do not face. Organizations must spend time with human resources tracking and reporting. Small organizations can accomplish this task with one HR manager or a few HR professionals. However, large organizations face an exponentially larger challenge. To scale up the solution would require an unmanageable number of HR employees. This is where software excels, especially specialized HR software. This chapter will cover Human Resource Information Systems (HRIS), Human Resource Management Systems (HRMS), and the effectiveness of this type of software.

What will be covered in this chapter

- Recruitment tracking

- Confidential personnel files

- Payroll management

- Benefits administration

- Learning and development

- Attendance management

- Performance management

Global organizations face the global challenges to manage and maintain human resource confidential data. The global company's product faces international competition. Globalizations allows companies to serve customers worldwide and be able to effectively manage product and resources at low costs. The terms global and international are used interchangeably. Domestic markets are when the products are made and sold in the same country. Global is when the company makes products in one country and sells them in another. Local responsiveness is extremely high with a global organization and a multi-location company looks at the world as its market. The education level in the countries where the company operates is an especially important topic for Human Resources professionals. When a business decides to expand to another region or country, the knowledge of the education, skills, abilities of that worker of that country will be an important aspect for the companies and their human resource professionals. Much of the human capital of the country depends on the qualified employee base of that country. Economics influences organizations and human resource dynamics; since the cost of labor varies in each country, it is an important element in strategic discussions of globalization. Human Resource Management from a global perspective has many key considerations. Before implementing the best practices of human resource management, identifying what works for a local entity and blending it in the overarching corporate umbrella is the key. Companies' overall strategy, human resource practices and implementation of the systems that align with each country is a major consideration in the business decision.

Competitive advantage and impact on the bottom-line results in an ever-changing environment are directly connected with the availability of the resources for the firm. One of the key issues of a successful human resource strategy is that, in recent years, it is greatly influenced by modern technology. Human Resource Information Systems (HRIS) basically record, store, collect, analyze, and retrieve the data of the organization's current and past employees. Many HRIS systems also integrate with applicant tracking systems to store, collect and analyze the data of the applicants interested in the organizations.

The HRIS system mainly eliminates the administrative paperwork and stores the information easily retrievable for the data reporting purposes. HRIS systems are used for many different purposes like using the data for reports, simplifying and accelerating the administrative process, paper free human resources, collecting and storing confidential information, controlling available data, minimizing labor costs, filing accurate reports with department of labor, and being able to provide the current data in a short time to make strategic business decisions related to human capital. Social and organizational changes are extremely broad in the financial environment. Concurrent to the financial environment, it is imperative for human resource management to be extremely broad and comprehensive, fast and flexible, and change with the adapting environment. Utilizing the data and communication technology with HRM that interacts with other financial systems helps the business leaders make the key decisions. Companies can track employment lifecycle for different types of employees ranging from exempt, nonexempt, independent contractors, gig workers, etc. As a result of this, human resource management professionals use the technology framework to support the future organization.

There are several terms used for Human Resources Management Systems. HRIS systems are implemented in organizations to enhance the HR departments and management can use the reporting to make key decisions. Effective Human Resource Management provides competitive advantage requiring accurate and updated information for current and potential employees in the labor market. Technology evolution has improvised new techniques to collect the right information through the development of HRIS systems. Usually HRIS includes systems and processes that connect and integrate with several other data systems in an organization. Global organizations choose to implement Human Resource Information Systems after they have established Enterprise Resource Planning Systems (ERPS) and Customer Relationship Management (CRM) system solutions, hoping to improve the processes associated with sales data, financial data, and employee related data.

The modern HR function is more strategic and less administrative. Administrative processes are mainly reduced by HRIS systems in different functions like recruitment, personnel files, labor reports, employee motivation, and shaping the organizational culture. With the help of these new systems, employees are able to control, monitor, and execute their development plans.

HRIS systems are able to provide strategic and forecasting information about the organization. Data collected with the HRIS systems provide a strong mechanism for the management decision. With efficient Human Resource Management Systems, companies are able to provide accurate data that will have consequences for the entire organization. There are many reports such as cost per employee, turnover rates, time to fill the position, overtime cost, overall labor costs, and return on the HR capital. Any HRIS system includes reporting functionalities; and many systems track applicants and employee information is interfaced with payroll systems. An HRIS system is specifically designed for management to support data driven decisions. Most HRIS contain personal history of employees, work history, pay history, job title, performance reviews history, training and development history, skills, competencies, and education history. The pressure is on Human Resources to embrace the technologies and contribute to the bottom line of the organization and improve the morale and efficiency of the employees. The typical HR professional is involved with many different flows of the work. HR is the gatekeeper for the information with the support of HRIS.

15.1 HRMS Effectiveness and Efficiencies

Human Resources Management Systems are capable of creating efficiencies by dramatically improving the level of service, reducing costs, and allowing HR professionals to dedicate more time to work on strategic projects. Many HRMS systems are implemented by cutting the HR staff and outsourcing most of the tasks. However, HR departments have increasingly developed efficiencies with the help of evolved HRMS systems. In most cases HRIS or HRMS systems contain these modules: attendance management, payroll management, recruitment and applicant tracking, learning and development, employee administration, management reporting, and employee self service.

Figure 15.1   **Sub-Modules of HRMS Systems**

15.2 Recruitment Tracking

Collecting all the applicants and monitoring all the recruitment efforts that allows the applicants to view and apply the positions of the organizations and HR organizations can collect and process the applications. Posting the jobs online and collecting the applications has become the standard protocol in many organizations. Once the applications are collected, employers will start pre-screening the received resumes. Companies also use this system to send Equal Employment Opportunity (EEO) reports to the Department of Labor, monitor the interview process and assign the interviewer, keep accurate statistics on the new hires, and transfer them to payroll systems.

15.3 Confidential Personnel Files

Keeping confidential personnel databases of all the employees is the compliance responsibility of the organization. It is especially important for an organization to have these data standardized. This module in HRIS systems includes personal employees, emergency contacts, wage history, absenteeism history, training and certifications received, disciplinary action, workers compensation information, etc.

15.4 Payroll

Payroll modules may or may not be part of the regular HRIS system. Many companies prefer to outsource payroll duties and keep them separate from the HRIS system for various reasons. One key reason is that global companies often want to integrate countries' HRIS systems but want to keep payroll systems separate due to local regulations. The payroll system automates the process by collecting the data on employee time and attendance, overtime report, calculate various state and federal taxes, generating periodic paychecks and employee tax reports. This system is mostly heavily integrated with the financial systems of the company.

15.5 Benefits Administration

HRIS systems provide administration of benefits integration. It integrates with various pension and insurance systems, which helps keep track of employee participation. Important and critical information such as pension plans, life insurance options, and employee stock options are all distributed through HRIS systems. Employees can make their required elections and keep track of their and employer contributions.

15.6 Learning and Development

Training new and existing employees is an integral part of employee performance management. Organizations invest in employees each year and it is important to keep track of all the training that employees have completed during their employment. Companies buy the Learning & Development module often called a Learning Management System (LMS) to keep track of all employee's education, qualifications, certifications, allowing storing various training, courses, lectures, etc. Online and virtual training libraries provide high flexibility and cost efficiency.

15.7 Performance Management

This module in HRIS tracks and documents all performance related measures for employees for continuous monitoring, evaluation, and reporting purposes. It is important to understand which objectives are met for any employees and which needs improvement. The performance management should not be taken as criticism but rather a positive improvement. The module contains many features including the monitoring of the performance tracking, embedded with the learning module for an employee and provides reminders and updates to managers and employees for timely completion of the review.

In addition to the above modules, HRIS systems have many different modules introduced lately. It takes the administrative aspect of the HR department away and creates more strategic scenarios where HR can track the gaps and address them with the leadership team. HRIS is a systemized approach to increase competitiveness by improving the administrative paperwork transactions in a HR department. It shifts the focus of the HR department from being very administrative to very strategic. It includes employee dialogues and two-way communication. For Management leaders, an HRIS increases the efficiency and the decision-making ability of the organization overall.

Quiz

1. **What does HRMS stand for?**

   a. Healthy Regional Market Solutions

   b. Human Resource Management System

   c. Human Resource Mutual Synergy

   d. Highly Rational Metaphor Study

2. **What does HRIS stand for?**

   a. Human Resource Information System

   b. Highly Reasonable Informative Students

   c. Human Resource Ideal Solution

   d. Headstrong Really Independent Students

3. **What does EEO stand for?**

   a. Equal Employment Opportunity

   b. Every Employee Overworks

   c. Equal Employee Oversight

   d. Equal Employment Observer

4. What does LMS stand for?

a. Learning Makes Sense

b. Leaders Make Solutions

c. Learning Management System

d. Learning Marketing Solutions

5. What does ERPS stand for?

a. Every Rapid Product Succeeds

b. Each Ratio Processes Sensibly

c. Enterprise Response Platform System

d. Enterprise Resource Planning System

6. What should global companies consider when hiring workers in another country?

a. Race or ethnicity

b. Sex, gender identity, orientation

c. Level of education and skills

d. Religious affiliation

7. Which of these is not a feature of HRIS?

a. Replaces old paper and file cabinets

b. Increases cost by 50%

c. Keeps employee information safe from fires and floods

d. Makes information available in different countries

8. **What types of employees can HRIS help companies track?**

   a. Exempt & non exempt

   b. Contractors

   c. Temporary

   d. All of the above

9. **Which of these cannot be tracked by standalone payroll companies?**

   a. Local, state, and federal taxes

   b. Overtime

   c. Attendance

   d. Inefficient workers

10. **Which of these cannot be tracked by an LMS?**

    a. Course completion

    b. Certifications

    c. Education

    d. Local taxes

Answers	1 – b	2 – a	3 – a	4 – c	5 – d
	6 – c	7 – b	8 – d	9 – d	10 – d

Chapter Summary

Global organizations face global competition. They are able to offer products in multiple markets, but each market has its own unique competitive challenges. Executive leadership must consider the readiness of local workers for the company's needs. Some regions have better levels of education and skills than others. It is important to only open a local branch of the company in an area that can sustain the human resource needs of the organization. The cost of labor is lower in some countries, but sometimes those regions have lower overall skills that the company needs. Human resource information systems (HRIS) integrate with applicant tracking systems to store and analyze data on past, current, and potential employees. HRIS replaces the old needs for paper and file cabinets and keeps the information safe from natural disasters such as fires and floods. Global organizations are able to access employee records in multiple countries, but must also keep those records safe and confidential. With HRIS, companies can track exempt, nonexempt, contract, and temporary workers. Many companies prefer to keep their payroll separate from their HRIS. Standalone payroll companies automatically calculate intricate details from different countries and process them instantly and accurately; this includes local, state, and federal taxes, overtime, and attendance. HRIS can integrate with benefits providers such as health insurance companies and pension providers. Rather than feel replaced and unnecessary, HR departments should embrace the efficiency and use their time to find gaps and address them with leadership.

Automation has often been seen as displacing workers, but there always seems to be another opportunity for employees.

Chapter 16

Assessments Used in Organizational Behavior

Organizational behavior assessments play a crucial role in deciphering the intricacies of workplace dynamics, employee interactions, and overall organizational effectiveness. In this chapter, we will explore the diverse range of assessments available to organizations, shedding light on their significance and application in the ever-evolving landscape of organizational behavior. When using assessments in organizational behavior, it is essential to ensure they are dependable, valid, and ethically administered. Additionally, interpreting results should consider the context of the organization and the individual(s) being assessed.

What will be covered in this chapter?

- The importance of assessments in organizational behavior for overall organizational health

- The difference between personality, behavioral, emotional intelligence, strengths and team assessments along with their uses

- The organizational and financial benefits that organizations receive by properly aligning their strategy, culture, and talent through insights gleaned from assessments

- An introduction to Belbin Team Roles

While there are many types of assessments, and an entire book can be written on this topic, we are going to focus on those assessments that impact organizational behavior from an individual, team, and organization level. These include:

- Surveys and Questionnaires

- Psychological, Cognitive, and Behavioral Assessments

- Team Assessments

- Organizational Effectiveness Assessments

16.1 Surveys and Questionnaires – Unveiling Organizational Insights

Organizational surveys are powerful tools that organizations use to gather systematic data and feedback from their employees, stakeholders, or other relevant groups. These surveys play a crucial role in assessing various aspects of the organization, understanding the perspectives of individuals within it, and informing strategic decision-making.

Organizational surveys are structured data collection methods designed to gather information about different facets of an organization. These surveys are characterized by their systematic approach, utilizing well-crafted questions and methodologies to gather insights. Organizational surveys serve multiple purposes including:

- **Assessment of employee engagement** – Gauging the level of engagement and satisfaction among employees

- **Evaluation of leadership effectiveness** – Assessing leadership styles and their impact on organizational culture

- **Identification of areas of improvement** – Pinpointing specific aspects of the organization that may need attention or enhancement

These surveys typically include components such as employee engagement, leadership and management, and organizational culture. Understanding the prevailing culture within an organization and its impact on employees is critical to understanding organizational behavior. Surveys can be conducted through various methodologies, including online surveys, paper-and-pencil surveys, interviews, or a combination of these. The methodology chosen often depends on factors such as the size of the organization, the nature of the questions, and the desired level of respondent anonymity.

Surveys are integral to the effective functioning and improvement of an organization. They assist in data-driven decision-making, employee voice, and continuous improvement. Organizational surveys provide data that facilitates evidence-based decision-making. The insights gleaned from surveys inform leaders about the current state of the organization, helping them make informed choices on strategies and interventions. Surveys provide a platform for employees to express their opinions, concerns, and suggestions. This contributes to a culture of openness and inclusion, where the diverse perspectives of individuals are valued. Finally, by regularly conducting surveys, organizations can track changes over time, identify trends, and continuously strive for improvement. The iterative process is crucial for staying responsive to evolving organizational needs.

While organizational surveys offer numerous benefits, they come with challenges that need careful consideration. Challenges include survey fatigue, ensuring anonymity and confidentiality, and collecting actionable insights. Frequent surveys can lead to survey fatigue, where employees become disengaged or less willing to participate. Organizations must strike a balance between collecting valuable data and respecting employees' time and attention. Maintaining respondent anonymity is critical to obtaining honest and open feedback. Organizations must establish clear protocols to ensure that survey responses are kept confidential, fostering trust among participants. Finally, collecting data is not enough. Organizations must be prepared to act on insights gleaned. Lack of action in response to survey results can lead to disillusionment among employees and diminish the effectiveness and trust of future surveys, or the change management resulting from survey learnings.

16.2 Personality, Behavioral, Emotional Intelligence, and Strengths Assessments

Behavioral assessments encompass a range of tools designed to evaluate, measure, and comprehend the behavioral patterns of individuals and groups within organizations. These assessments go beyond traditional performance metrics, delving into the psychological and emotional dimensions that influence individual behaviors impacting workplace dynamics. There are many types of personality, cognitive, and behavioral assessments. They include:

- Personality assessments– Uncover the unique traits and characteristics that shape individual behavior. Examples include the Myers-Briggs Type Indicator (MBTI) and the Big Five Personality Traits model.

- Behavioral assessments– Identify how individuals will react to environmental stimuli. Examples include DISC and the Enneagram.

- Emotional intelligence assessments – Measure an individual's ability to understand, manage, and navigate one's emotions and enhance leadership development potential through interpersonal effectiveness.

- Strengths assessments – Measure positive strengths and talents, natural aptitudes, personal preferences, and areas for professional development.

There are many benefits to the insights gleaned from personality and behavioral assessments. First is their involvement in talent management, especially talent acquisition and development. These insights assist leaders in identifying candidates with the right behavioral fit for specific roles or tailoring development programs to enhance individual and team behaviors. They also influence talent acquisition and recruiting efforts using behavioral-based questions.

While each assessment has its own definition, purpose, and best use, it is recommended to glean insights from a multitude of assessments to get a holistic picture of strengths and blind spots across individuals, teams, and organizations for effective leadership development and training. Below is a list of the most used assessments, their purpose, and their best use.

16.2.1 Personality and Behavioral

1. **Myers-Briggs Type Indicator (MBTI):**

   a. Definition: Classifies individuals into 16 personality types based on preferences in four dichotomies (e.g., extraversion/introversion).

   b. Best use: Team building, communication improvement, career advancement

2. **Big Five Personality Traits:**

   a. Definition: Measures personality based on five traits — openness, conscientiousness, extraversion, agreeableness, and neuroticism.

   b. Best use: Hiring decision, team dynamics, personal development

3. **DISC Assessment:**

   a. Definition: Categorizes individuals into four personality types — Dominance, Influence, Steadiness, and Conscientiousness.

   b. Best use: Communication improvement, conflict resolution, team building

4. **16 PF (Sixteen Personality Factor Questionnaire):**

   a. Definition: Measures 16 primary personality factors, providing a detailed personality profile.

   b. Best use: Psychological research, career counseling, leadership development

5. **Enneagram:**

   a. Definition: Classifies individuals into nine personality types based on their core motivations and fears.

   b. Best use: Self-awareness, personal development, conflict resolution

6. **Kiersey Temperament Sorter:**

   a. Definition: A variant of MBTI that classifies individuals into four temperaments – Artisan, Guardian, Idealist, and Rationalist.

   b. Best use: Team dynamics, communication improvement, personal development

7. **Predictive Index (PI):**

   a.   Definition: Assesses workplace behavior and cognitive ability to predict job performance. It identifies individuals' motivating drives and needs.

   b.   Best use: Employee selection, talent management, team dynamics, and workforce planning

Personality and behavioral assessments hold significant benefits for both organizational behavior and leadership development, contributing to a more nuanced understanding of individuals and teams within an organization.

As you can see in their best uses above, in the realm of organizational behavior, these assessments play a pivotal role in enhancing self-awareness among employees. By shedding light on an individual's unique personality traits and behavioral tendencies, these assessments empower employees to recognize their strengths, preferences, and areas for development. This heightened self-awareness forms the basis for improved interpersonal relationships and effective communication within teams.

Organizations that integrate personality and behavioral assessments often witness improved team dynamics, since teams are composed of individuals with diverse personalities and behavioral styles, and understanding, navigating, and valuing these differences enhances teamwork and collaboration. Understanding the varied approaches that team members bring to tasks and challenges promotes a culture of mutual respect and cooperation, contributing to a more cohesive and high-performing team.

In the realm of leadership development, personality and behavioral assessment offer a roadmap for the basis of talent development and succession planning. Understanding one's leadership styles, strengths, and potential blind spots provides a foundation for targeted personal and professional development efforts. Managers and leaders armed with insights into their own personalities and those of their team members can tailor the development plans to align the needs of their teams and the organization, fostering more effective and adaptive leadership styles.

In addition, behavioral assessments may uncover patterns of productive and nonconstructive behaviors impacting effective communication, decision-making, and teamwork. Managers and leaders who recognize these tendencies are better positioned to guide their organizations through change.

Understanding personality and behavioral profiles also influences organizational behavior through leadership development and cultural enhancement. Insights gleaned from assessments inform opportunities to enhance leadership effectiveness by understanding and developing key behavioral and leadership competencies. Additionally, they help align individual and group behaviors with desired cultural values, driving cultural transformation initiatives. Finally, assessments improve team optimization by identifying and addressing effective behavioral dynamics within and across teams. They improve communication, collaboration, and overall team performance.

Behavioral assessments offer a strategic lens through which organizations can optimize their most valuable asset

– their people. By leveraging these assessments thoughtfully, organizations can unlock the potential for enhanced collaboration, improved performance, and a workplace culture that aligns with the ever-evolving demands of the modern business landscape.

16.2.2 Emotional Intelligence Assessments

1. **Emotional Intelligence Appraisal (EQ-I 2.0):**

   a. Definition: Measures emotional intelligence across five composite scales – Self-perception, self-expression, interpersonal, decision-making, and stress management.

   b. Best use: Leadership development, personal growth, team collaboration

2. **Emotional Competence Inventory (ECI) and Emotional Social Competence Inventory (ESCI):**

   a. Definition: Developed by Daniel Goleman and Richard Boyatzis, assesses emotional and social competencies/ intelligence in the workplace through 12 competencies.

   b. Best use: Leadership development, team effectiveness, organizational performance, and cultural improvement

3. **Mayer-Salovey-Caruso Emotional Intelligence Test (MSCEIT):**

   a. Definition: Assesses emotional intelligence by measuring four branches – Perceiving emotions, using emotions to facilitate thought, understanding emotions, and managing emotions.

b. Best use: Leadership development, interpersonal effectiveness, organizational training

4. **Bar-On Emotional Quotient Inventory (EQ-i):**

   a. Definition: Assesses emotional and social functioning across various subscales, providing an overall emotional quotient (EQ) score.

   b. Best use: Personal development, leadership coaching, team dynamics

Emotional Intelligence (EI) assessments offer invaluable insights into the realm of organizational behavior and leadership development. Combined with insights gleaned from personality and behavioral assessments, they assist managers and leaders in creating a more harmonious and effective workplace culture. Emotional Intelligence assessment dives into an individual's capacity to recognize, understand, and manage their emotions and respond to how their actions may have impacted team members.

In context to organizational behavior, the benefits of emotional intelligence assessments lay the foundation for enhancing self-awareness, which is foundational to leadership capability. Those who are vulnerable and have the capability and capacity to understand their own emotions and their impact on behavior are better equipped to navigate working relationships and the workplace. This heightened awareness fosters a culture of trust and psychological safety, where all individuals can authentically express themselves, creating an open and communicative environment where unique perspectives are appreciated, respected, and valued.

When combined with personality and behavioral assessments, emotional intelligence assessments also facilitate the foundation for improved people skills, leading to better levels of collaboration and communication, and fostering a greater sense of respect, trust, and safety in the workplace. This positive cultural dynamic contributes to a more cohesive and motivated workforce, driving the overall success and performance of the organization.

In leadership development, emotional intelligence and self-awareness represent the foundation for effective leadership. Leaders with strong EI skills inspire confidence, gain trust, motivate teams, and create a positive culture. These leaders exhibit flexibility, adaptability, and resiliency in the face of change, foundational skills for all team members in navigating barriers impacting the business.

16.2.3 Strengths Assessments

1. **StrengthsFinder (CliftonStrengths):**

   a. Definition: Identifies and ranks an individual's top strengths out of 34 possibilities.

   b. Best use: Personal development, team roles, leadership

2. **Strengths-Based Leadership:**

   a. Definition: Focuses on identifying and leveraging individuals and team strengths for leadership development, primarily through a competency model (e.g., Korn Ferry, PDI, Global Novations).

   b. Best use: Leadership training, team building, organizational development

3. VIA Survey of Character Strengths:

a. Definitions: Focuses on 24-character strengths grouped under six virtues.

b. Best use: Personal growth, coaching, positive psychology interventions

Like personality, behavioral, and emotional intelligence assessments, strengths-based assessments also offer unique insights that shape organizational behavior and leadership development. In the realm of organizational behavior, strengths-based assessments provide individuals with an understanding of their strengths and blind spots, knowing what skills and behaviors to scale, and which to develop. Individuals, managers, and leaders gain insights into what they naturally excel at and where their unique talents lie. Allowing employees to capitalize on their strengths on the job increases job satisfaction and higher levels of employee engagement.

Teams within organizations benefit significantly from a strengths-based approach. By recognizing and leveraging the diverse strengths of team members, teams become more collaborative and effective. Everyone is in flow and this approach encourages a culture where individuals appreciate and celebrate each other's contributions.

Talent management is another area positively influenced by strengths-based assessments. Organizations can strategically place individuals within roles that align with their strengths, maximizing organizational impact and job satisfaction, and driving overall success within the organization. Additionally, as part of talent management, succession planning within the organization is streamlined by identifying and nurturing the leadership strengths and competencies necessary for advancement within the organization. Building a talent development strategy grounded in organizational strengths and competencies aligned with expected organizational behaviors and core values drives organizational effectiveness.

Pulling It All Together

The integration of insights from personality, behavioral, emotional intelligence, and strengths-based assessments forms a powerful synergy that significantly enhances organizational behavior, leadership development, and contributes to a competitive advantage within the business landscape. Building a high-performing culture of skilled talent requires the insights gleaned from such assessments.

Research from LSA Global shows that companies that align their culture and talent with their corporate strategy drive peak performance and outperform their peers across many critical financial and leadership metrics.

Figure 16.1   **LSA 3X Organizational Alignment Research: Aligned Companies Significantly Outperform Their Peers**

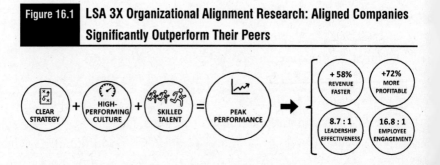

Financially, revenues are generated 58% faster and companies aligning these key attributes are 72% more profitable. Additionally, aligned companies have 16.8x greater levels of employee engagement and 8.7x greater levels of leadership effectiveness. Beyond these metrics, both customer satisfaction and retention are higher in aligned organizations by 3.2x and 2.2x respectively.

In the realm of organizational behavior, the collective insights from these assessments foster a deep understanding of individuals and teams. Personality assessments unveil the intrinsic traits that shape behavior, while behavioral assessments illuminate patterns of actions and reactions. Emotional intelligence assessments provide a nuanced understanding of how individuals navigate and manage emotions, contributing to improved interpersonal dynamics. Simultaneously, strengths-based assessments shed light on individual and team strengths, creating a positive framework for collaboration.

The combined insights from these assessments empower employees to navigate workplace interactions with self-awareness, communicate effectively, and contribute positively to team dynamics. Teams, equipped with knowledge about each other's personalities, behaviors, emotional intelligence, and strengths, form a cohesive unit that celebrates diversity, encourages open communication, and transforms conflicts into opportunities for growth.

Organizations obtaining insights from these assessments and integrating them into talent management strategy create a high-performing culture that is deliberate and disciplined in upskilling and reskilling its talent. Organizations that scale their leadership competencies outperform their competition and drive more predictable and sustainable results.

16.3 Team and Organizational Effectiveness Assessments

Teams serve as fundamental building blocks within organizations. They are responsible for performing the actions and tactics necessary to execute the strategies of an organization and deliver company objectives and goals. Understanding the dynamics of teams is paramount for organizational success. Team assessments play a pivotal role in unraveling the complexities of teamwork, offering insights into team dynamics, strengths, and areas for improvement. These assessments gauge various dimensions, such as communication, collaboration, and individual contributions. The primary objectives of team assessments include:

- Performance optimization – Identifying factors that contribute to or hinder team performance

- Communication enhancement – Evaluating the quality and effectiveness of communication within the team.

- Roles and Responsibilities – Clarifying roles and responsibilities to ensure a well-defined and efficient workflow.

- Conflict resolution – Pinpointing sources of conflict and implementing strategies for resolution

While insights may be gleaned in aggregate from the personality and behavioral assessments mentioned above, there are specific team-based assessments that allow leaders to drive greater effectiveness within their organizations – group dynamics, team effectiveness, cultural influences, motivating values, and conflict resolutions.

One of the most famous and widely used team assessments is Patrick Lencioni's 5 Dysfunctions of a Team. This model looks at five key areas of team performance.

- Team Trust – How well team members trust one another and the willingness to admit mistakes, acknowledge weaknesses, or ask for help (authenticity and vulnerability)

- Conflict – Does the team allow healthy conflict to drive effective team processes? Constructive conflict allows team members to share ideas and perspectives, increasing the potential for better decision-making

- Commitment – Do team members buy into the big picture? Is there a clear vision of the overall objective and an individual understanding of how contributions fit into the achievement of objectives?

- Accountability – Accountability for actions hinges on how committed team members feel within the organization. Are team members valued for the unique skills that they bring to the organization?

- Intention of Results – What is the overall objective? Are teams focused on the bigger picture or are they sidetracked by individual or team results at the expense of the organization?

Figure 16.2 | **Patrick Lencioni's Five Dysfunctions of a Team**

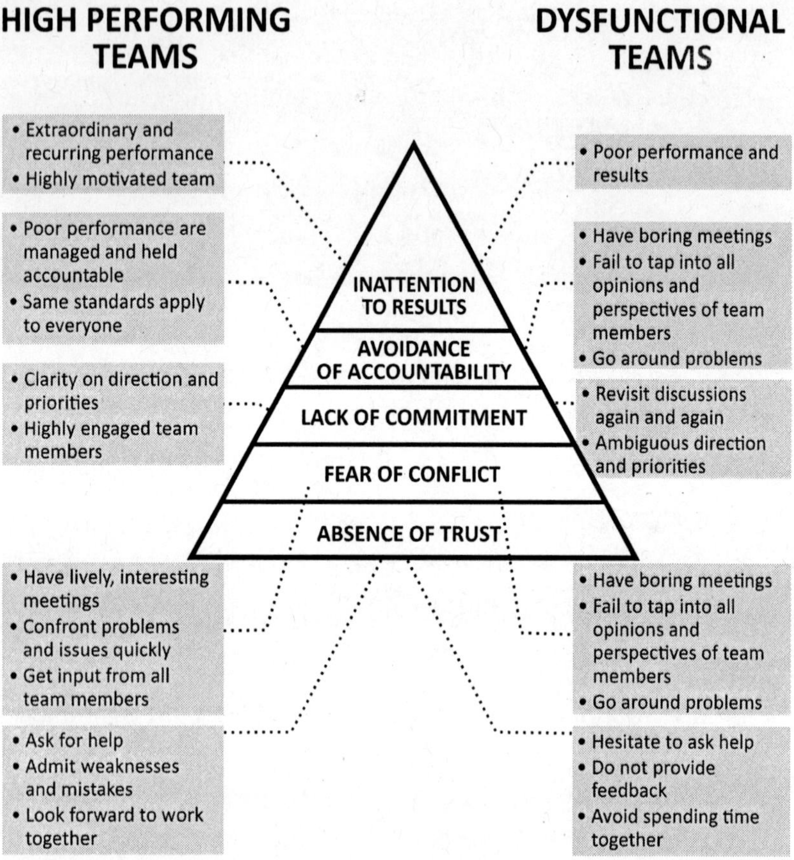

HIGH PERFORMING TEAMS

DYSFUNCTIONAL TEAMS

- Extraordinary and recurring performance
- Highly motivated team

- Poor performance and results

- Poor performance are managed and held accountable
- Same standards apply to everyone

INATTENTION TO RESULTS

- Have boring meetings
- Fail to tap into all opinions and perspectives of team members
- Go around problems

AVOIDANCE OF ACCOUNTABILITY

- Clarity on direction and priorities
- Highly engaged team members

LACK OF COMMITMENT

- Revisit discussions again and again
- Ambiguous direction and priorities

FEAR OF CONFLICT

ABSENCE OF TRUST

- Have lively, interesting meetings
- Confront problems and issues quickly
- Get input from all team members

- Have boring meetings
- Fail to tap into all opinions and perspectives of team members
- Go around problems

- Ask for help
- Admit weaknesses and mistakes
- Look forward to work together

- Hesitate to ask help
- Do not provide feedback
- Avoid spending time together

The behaviors of organizations are grounded in the behaviors of their teams and people. Effective teams utilize the various personality types of their members. Some individuals are more effective in thought-oriented or results-oriented roles, while others may excel in people-oriented or organizational-oriented roles. Understanding these different preferences and strengths helps optimize the makeup of teams to leverage the collective strengths of its members. The Belbin Team Inventory was first introduced in 1981 to measure these preferences.

In optimizing Organizational Behavior and effectiveness, the Belbin Team Inventory identifies nine roles[7]:

Thought-Oriented

- Monitors – Make decisions based on facts as opposed to emotions and instincts

- Specialists – Experts in their respective fields with in-depth knowledge of a subject matter

- Plants – Free-thinkers and creatives who challenge paradigms, produce original ideas, and suggest innovative ways of completing tasks

Action-Oriented

- Shapers – Extroverts who motivate themselves and others to achieve results

- Implementers – Organizers who structure their environments and maintain order

- Completers/Finishers –Those who perform quality assurance during key stages of a project

People-Oriented

- Coordinators – Possess excellent interpersonal and communication skills and help team members accomplish individual goals and objectives

- Team Workers – Extroverts with friendly dispositions that assist the team in functioning as a unit

- Resource Investigators – Those with a talent for networking and skilled at gaining insights and ideas from others, sharing them with other key stakeholders

---

7. "The Nine Belbin Team Roles." https://www.belbin.com.

Two additional team assessments worth mentioning that drive operational effectiveness and improve organizational behavior are Culture Pulse and Motivating Values.

As defined by global assessment provider Cloverleaf, the Culture Pulse assessment measures values, norms, beliefs, and behavior, and demonstrates how culture controls the way employees behave amongst themselves as well as with people outside the organization. The Motivating Values assessment measures the primary influences in a person's life, which initiate and stimulate behavior. Some values are assigned great worth and are sought diligently. Others are not considered important and may be ignored. Values are fundamental incentives to motivation. An individual's primary values will cause the where and why a person behaves the way they do, but not the how. Both Culture Pulse and Motivating Value reveal the influences and motivations of individuals, which may impact their collaboration on teams.

Quiz

1. **Personality and behavioral assessments measure the same things.**

   a. True

   b. False

2. **What assessment can share results to enhance an individual's leadership potential through greater interpersonal effectiveness?**

   a. Myers-Briggs Type Indicator

   b. Enneagram

   c. Emotional Intelligence

   d. DISC

   e. None of the above

3. **What benefits do surveys and questionnaires have for organizations?**

   a. Gauge the level of engagement and satisfaction in employees

   b. Assess leadership styles and effectiveness

   c. Pinpoints strengths and weaknesses

   d. All of the above

   e. None of the above

4. **What are some potential issues with surveys?**

   a. Survey fatigue

   b. No real data to inform actional insights

   c. Anonymity and confidentiality

   d. A and B

   e. A and C

5. **Which one of the following is not a benefit from learnings gained from team and organizational assessments:**

   a. Communication

   b. Confrontation

   c. Collaboration

   d. Contribution

   e. None of the above

6. **The 5 Dysfunctions of a team include:**

   a. Trust, Culture, Collaboration, Accountability, Intention of Results

   b. Teamwork, Culture, Commitment, Action, Intention of Results

   c. Trust, Conflict, Commitment, Accountability, Inspiration

   d. Trust, Conflict, Commitment, Accountability, Intention of Results

   e. None of the above

7. Having boring meetings, failing to tap into all opinions and perspectives of team members, and go around problems is which stage of the 5 Dysfunctions of the Team?

   a. Trust

   b. Conflict

   c. Commitment

   d. Accountability

   e. B and D

8. Clarity on direction and priorities and highly engaged team members are at what stage of the Lencioni pyramid of high-performing teams?

   a. Trust

   b. Conflict

   c. Commitment

   d. Accountability

   e. Results

9. The three categories of Belbin Team Roles are:

   a. Thought-Oriented, Results-Oriented, Self-Oriented

   b. Task-Oriented, Action-Oriented, Self-Oriented

   c. Task-Oriented, Results-Oriented, People-Oriented

   d. Thought-Oriented, Action-Oriented, People-Oriented

   e. None of the above

10. Freethinkers and creative people who produce original ideas and suggest innovative ways of completing tasks are known as:

   a. Monitors

   b. Shapers

   c. Implementers

   d. Coordinators

   e. Plants

Answers	1 – b	2 – c	3 – d	4 – e	5 – b
	6 – d	7 – e	8 – c	9 – d	10 – e

Chapter Summary

While organizational analysis has been around for over 20 years, it has mostly been connected to restructuring efforts and some change management initiatives. However, with the rise of data, predictive and prescriptive analytics, and artificial intelligence, organizational analysis is deemed a priority in organizational behavior, especially in today's workplace, where employee engagement and job satisfaction are at an all-time low. Retaining and training employees is more cost-effective than competing for talent. Determining whether to upskill, reskill, or hire for skills has a significant fiscal impact on organizations.

Thriving workplace cultures and organizations support employee engagement and employee development. Today's workplace is complicated and the residual impacts of the COVID-19 pandemic on the workplace remain significant. Leaders must navigate the ever-changing landscape of their organizations to increase employee engagement and job satisfaction.

Research findings from the Human Capital Institute (HCI) and the International Coaching Federation (ICF) found that:

◆ 54% of high-performing organizations are classified as coaching organizations

◆ 45% of employees surveyed said they will "definitely" or "probably" move to an external organization

◆ Only 33% of men and 24% of women believe that leadership cares about their career development and opportunities

◆ Only 33% of men and 21% of women believe that leadership is focused on their skills development to help them in their careers

These are sobering statistics. Organizational assessments can provide insights to assist leaders in increasing levels of employee engagement and satisfaction. Organizational assessments provide critical insights for leaders to understand their employees, teams, and organization's strengths and blind spots. Research shows that using assessments to assess organizational health and, in turn, aligning an organization's culture and talent with its corporate strategy increases financial metrics such as revenue and profit growth, while at the same time, its leadership effectiveness and employee engagement.

Team and organizational effectiveness assessments offer a multitude of benefits that significantly impact organizational behavior and invaluable tools to contribute to the development of a thriving workplace. By understanding and leveraging the insight gained from these assessments, organizations can enhance collaboration, leadership effectiveness, and overall organizational behavior, leading to sustained success and growth.

Glossary

ADDIE – Analysis, Design, Development, Implementation, Evaluation - This is a process for creating training programs from start to finish.

CBT – Computer-Based Training (see also WBT) - Training that can be completed on a computer. This is often used interchangeably with, but is subtly different from, WBT because the training module may be on a particular computer and not on the world wide web.

CEO – Chief Executive Officer - The highest ranking executive in an organization, usually a business.

CRM – Customer Relationship Management - A combination of practices, technologies, and strategies used to analyze and manage customer information and interactions usually in an effort to improve customer retention and sales growth.

EEO – Equal Employment Opportunity - This refers to organizations who commit to obeying the federal laws enforced by the EEOC. For example, "an equal opportunity employer."

EEOC – Equal Employment Opportunity Commission - A US agency dedicated to equality of opportunity for all job seekers regardless of classifications such as race, color, religion, sex, orientation, national origin, disaiblity, or genetic information.

ERPS – Enterprise Resource Planning System - Software used to manage daily activities like project management, compliance, and accounting.

FG – Facilitator Guide - Similar to a Participant Guide (PG), this document also includes notes for facilitators or trainers.

HPWS – High-Performance Work System - Practices used to improve employee effectiveness including recruiting, hiring, training, and compensation.

HR – Human Resources - Professionals who manage the information related to employees and bridge the gap between executives and employees/entry-level management.

HRIS – Human Resource Information System - see HRMS.

HRM – Human Resource Management - The practice of recruiting, hiring, and managing employees (see HR).

HRMS – Human Resource Management System - Software used for tracking and managing all of an organization's HR information including payroll, benefits, attendance, and training.

IDD – Instructional Designer/Developer - A professional, usually an individual contributor, who meets with managers, subject matter experts (SME) and front line workers to gather information then design and develop training materials in multiple media such as print, online, interactive eLearning, passive videos, tip sheets, SOEs, training manuals, user manuals, PGs, FGs, PowerPoint presentations, etc.

ILT – Instructor-Led Training - A training method in which a course is facilitated by an instructor or trainer; this can be in a physical classroom or auditorium, in a virtual or online classroom, or another method of live communication where the learner can hear the instructor and the instructor can interact with learners as they complete the course. This often relies heavily on lecture as the main method of delivering information.

Kirkpatrick Model – A four-stage method for evaluating training effectiveness consisting of reaction, learning, behavior, and evaluation.

L&D – Learning and Development - A branch of study including training, learning, talent development, and other methods for improving individuals, groups, and organizations.

LMS – Learning Management System - A repository, usually online software, for training curricula, individual courses, etc., that often also includes other features like goal, course completion, and compliance tracking.

OJT – On-the-Job Training - This is a method of training where a new employee is put to work immediately usually with a more experienced worker nearby to answer questions, offer suggestions, and lend support.

PG – Participant Guide - This is like a training manual or a shorter textbook. It often contains pictures, illustrations, screenshots, descriptions, and steps that help a participant learn specific content.

SOE – Sequence of Events - This document is a list of steps in a specific order usually with pictures, illustrations, or screenshots next to each step to help readers understand the process.

SWOT – Strengths, Weaknesses, Opportunities, and Threats - This is a method for evaluating a group or organization compared to itself (strengths and weaknesses) and compared to other organizations or the market at large (opportunities and threats).

T3 (or TTT) – Train-The-Trainer - This is a meeting or complete training program designed to prepare trainers for an upcoming course they will facilitate.

WBT – Web-Based Training (see also CBT) - Training that can be completed on the world wide web. This is often used interchangeably with, but is subtly different from, CBT because the training module may be accessed on any internet-capable device such as a smartphone or tablet and does not need to be completed on a computer.

Bibliography

Nancy J Adler – Global Dimensions of Organizational Behavior

Li, G., & Zhou, H. (2015). Globalization of financial capitalism and its impact on financial sovereignty. World Review of Political Economy, 6(2), 176-191

Daniel, S. J., Cieslewicz, J. K., & Pourjalali, H. (2012). The impact of national economic culture and country-level institutional environment on corporate governance practices. Management International Review, 52(3), 365-394. Derungs, I. M. (2011). Trans-cultural leadership for transformation. Basingstoke, England: Palgrave Macmillan

Bishop, W. H. (2013). The Elements of Leadership in a Global Environment. Global Business & Organizational Excellence, 32(5), 78-85.

Matveev & Nelson, 2004

Marquardt & Hovarth, 2001

Goffee & Jones, 1995

Kieffer, 1997

McEntee & Thornton, 1996

Bob Johansen (Leaders Make the Future)

Adrian Done (Global Trends)

Organization, behavior and culture, James Gibson, John Ivancevich, James Donnelly Jr., Robert Konopaske

Walmart 2016 Diversity Report

Inclusion by Jennifer Brown

Generational Diversity by Jamie Notter

7 Habits Of Highly Effective People. (2017). Simon & Schuster.

Babcock, L., Loewenstein, G., & Issacharoff, S. (1997). Creating Convergence: Debiasing Biased Litigants. Law & Social Inquiry, 22(04), 913-925. doi:10.1111/j.1747-4469.1997.tb01092.x

Boxall, P., & Macky, K. (2007). High-performance work systems and organisational performance: Bridging theory and practice. Asia Pacific Journal of Human Resources, 45(3), 261-270. doi:10.1177/1038411107082273.

Design Thinking and Implications for Organizational Design. (2020). Encyclopedia of Electronic HRM, 99-106. doi:10.1515/9783110633702-016

Globalization of Technologies. (n.d.). Introduction to Globalization and Business: Relationships and Responsibilities, 320-345. doi:10.4135/9781446215869.n11

Good to great: Why some companies make the leap ... and others don't by Jim Collins: Key takeaways, analysis & review. (2015). Instaread.

Harris, P. (2020). Maslow, Abraham (1908–1970) and Hierarchy of Needs. The Palgrave Encyclopedia of Interest Groups, Lobbying and Public Affairs, 1-3. doi:10.1007/978-3-030-13895-0_171-1

How to Avoid Rushing to Solutions When Problem-Solving. (2020, December 08). Retrieved from https://hbr.org/2020/11/how-to-avoid-rushing-to-solutions-when-problem-solving

Inclusion & Diversity. (n.d.). Retrieved from https://www.apple.com/diversity/

Inclusion Report 2020: Part of the Global Leadership Forecast series. (n.d.). Retrieved from https://www.ddiworld.com/research/inclusion-report

Leadership Development Shouldn't Be Left to Chance. (2020, November 16). Retrieved from https://www.td.org/professional-partner-content/leadership-development-shouldnt-be-left-to-chance

Leadership Skills: Problem-Solving. (2020). doi:10.4135/9781529719888

Levine, S. R. (2020, January 15). Diversity Confirmed To Boost Innovation And Financial Results. Retrieved from https://www.forbes.com/sites/forbesinsights/2020/01/15/diversity-confirmed-to-boost-innovation-and-financial-results/?sh=6d8c112bc4a6

LinkedIn's 2018 Workplace Learning Report. (n.d.). Retrieved from https://learning.linkedin.com/resources/workplace-learning-report-2018

Nathan, A. (2018, April 11). 7 Key Steps for Better Training and Development Programs. Retrieved from https://www.shrm.org/resourcesandtools/hr-topics/organizational-and-employee-development/pages/key-steps-for-better-training-development-programs.aspx

Pinder, C. C. (n.d.). Expectancy Theory of Work Motivation. Encyclopedia of Industrial and Organizational Psychology. doi:10.4135/9781412952651.n91

Shrm. (2019, October 10). Developing Employees. Retrieved from https://www.shrm.org/resourcesandtools/tools-and-samples/toolkits/pages/developingemployees.aspx

Thompson, L., & Loewenstein, G. (1992). Egocentric interpretations of fairness and interpersonal conflict. Organizational Behavior and Human Decision Processes, 51(2), 176-197. doi:10.1016/0749-5978(92)90010-5

Thompson, T., FS Flavio Silva, & Pereira, E. (2020, July 28). Ask Outcome-Focused Questions, Not Tool-Focused Questions. Retrieved from https://www.td.org/insights/ask-outcome-focused-questions-not-tool-focused-questions

Kurt, S. "Kirkpatrick Model: Four Levels of Learning Evaluation," in Educational Technology, October 24, 2016. Retrieved from https://educationaltechnology.net/kirkpatrick-model-four-levels-learning-evaluation/

"Definition of CHANGE," March 15, 2024. https://www.merriam-webster.com/dictionary/change.

Murphy, Mark. "The Big Reason Why Some People Are Terrified Of Change (While Others Love It)." Forbes. https://www.forbes.com/sites/markmurphy/2016/08/14/the-big-reason-why-some-people-are-terrified-of-change-while-others-love-it/.

Deloitte Insights. "2024 Global Human Capital Trends." https://www2.deloitte.com/us/en/insights/focus/human-capital-trends.html.

Harvard Business Review, Organizations Can't Change if Leaders Can't Change with Them, https://hbr.org/2016/10/organizations-cant-change-if-leaders-cant-change-with-them

Project Management Institute, https://www.pmi.org/

Hallio, https://haiilo.com/blog/the-2020-guide-to-organizational-change-management-ocm/

Prosci | The Global Leader in Change Management Solutions, https://www.prosci.com/

The Nine Belbin Team Roles, Belbin, https://www.belbin.com/about/belbin-team-roles

Notes